TO
MY TEACHER
KRUSHNA PRASAD MISHRA

THE CONCEPT OF PURUSA AND PURUSOTTAMA IN THE COMMENTARY OF SANKARA ON THE PRASTHANATRAYI

BY

PHANI MOHANTY

DEPARTMENT OF PHILOSOPHY. UTKAL UNIVERSITY

GYAN

ISBN : 978-81-212-1436-0

Published, 2018

Published by

Gyan Publishing House
5, Ansari Road
Daryaganj, New Delhi-110002
Phone: 011-47034999, 9811692060
www.gyanbooks.com
E-mail: books@gyanbooks.com

Printed at: G. Print Process, Delhi.

PREFACE

I am a Philosophy teacher since 1967. But temperamentally I am a poet and have been writing poetry since my school days. Like the mataphysical poets of Panchasakha period in Medieval Oriya Literature I have been drawn by the halo and glory of Lord Jagannātha—the Puruṣottama in my poetry. I developed a desire to unravel the mystery surrounding Lord Jagannātha—His Cult and Philosophy after I became a student of Philosophy. I read with avowed interest works of Pt. Neelakantha Das, Prof. B.M. Padhi, Prof. K.C. Mishra and Dr. H. K. Mahatab. These works are primarily historical, sociological and speculative. I wanted to study certain fundamental concepts like Puruṣa and Puruṣottama applying the modern analytical techneque.

Puruṣa and Puruṣottama concepts are dominant in the Gītā. I made an appeal to trace out the origin of these concepts and similar concepts in the Upaniṣads and Brahma-Sūtra and to throw light on interrelationship of these concepts in Indian Philosophical Literature. I think research in Indian Philosophical topics in modern times should be done in this way. It is possible that many readers and scholars may not agree with some of my observations and methods I have applied, but if the work provokes further examination and discussion I would feel amply rewarded.

Many logical issues are discussed in Indian Philosophy in the garb of theological and metaphysical trappings. Puruṣa and Puruṣottama concepts are very important. When analysed they unfold a definite view on causality to be found in the Prasthānatraya. The ambiguous use of these terms in the Prasthānatraya has been elaborately discussed in my work. In the introductory chapter, a brief history of the concepts of Puruṣa and Puruṣottama as found in the Indian Philosophical Literature has been discussed. The phenomenal world including all creatures are taken to be *Vyakta* by the Upaniṣads and the *Pradhhāna* by the Brahma-Sūtra and *Sarva bhūtāni* by the Gītā. "*Sarva bhūtāni*" really includes both matter and mind constituting the phenomenal world. This is the world of effects. Tracing its cause to akṣara, the Upaniṣads have discussed the concepts of Nirguṇa Brahman (*akṣara*$_1$), *māyā-śakti* (*akṣara*$_2$) and *Praṇava* (*akṣara*$_3$). But the causal chain does not stop with *akṣara*. It has been further traced back to the First Cause which is the Puruṣottama. The Puruṣottama is taken as '*Tajjalān*', '*Maheśvara*' and '*Dahara Puruṣa*' by the Upaniṣads, as '*Īśvara*' by the Brahma-Sūtra and as 'Vāsudeva' by the Bhagvat Gītā.

. The causal chain traced up to the Puruṣottama points out to Satkāryavāda, the theory of casuality; Śaṅkara's Vivartavāda as theory of causality is justified connecting the whole causal link from akṣara to Puruṣottma on the one hand and to the Nirguṇa Brahman on the other. When viewed in this way Nirguṇa Brahman becomes the *Adhiṣṭhana* on which the whole of phenomena including Īśvara has been superimposed. In this connection, the present work discusses nature of the two Brahmans, nature of causality, nature of Dahara Ākāśa and the concept of Highest Ethical Person.

While dealing with the language in which the logical issue of casuality has been put forward in the Prasthānatraya and Śaṅkara's commentry on it, the work also enumerates the characteristics of the Puruṣottama. Uttama is not ethical excellence but it is used in a sense of absolutely real *Vastu-Sat*. And in this sense the word Puruṣottma has been used. Īśvara is *Vastu-Sat* possessing the *Śakti*. He causes the other two Puruṣas to come with existence. Other synonyms of the Puruṣottama in the philosophical literature are 'Sanātanapuruṣa', 'Ādya Puruṣa' and 'Puruṣa Purāna'. But they are philosophically not as important as the term Puruṣottama.

Applying the contemporary analytical technique to duscuss the above mentioned concepts was a difficult task for me. I had to bank upon Śaṅkara's commentary on the Prasthānatraya in the absence of "Ordinary language" in India for discussing philosophical concepts. I assumed language used in the original commentary to be the "ordinary language" in this case.

P.M.

ACKNOWLEDGEMENT

I must first express my gratitude to may teacher and Guide Dr. K.P. Mishra, Dept. of Philosophy, Utkal University under whose supervision, the present work has been done.

My acknowledgements are also due to the University Grants Commission, New Delhi for awarding me the Teacher Fellowship for a period of three years and the Department of Education and Youth Services, Govt. of Orissa for permitting me duty leave for this period. I am also thankful to Dr. G. Mishra, Retd. Professor, Utkal University, Prof. G.C. Nayak, Head of the Department, of Philosophy, Utkal University, Prof. N.C. Panda, O.U.A.T., Bhubaneswar, Dr. G. Mishra, Reader in English, Utkal University and late M.S. Mohanty, Cuttack for their valuable help in preparing this work, I thank Mr. L. Palai for typing the thesis carefully.

I would also like to express my gratitude to many authors and scholars from whose works I have so extensively drawn materials for my work.

P.M.

LIST OF ABBREVIATIONS

AĀ	Aitareyāraṇyaka
AiU	Aitareyopaniṣad
AS	Ahirbudhnya Saṃhitā
AV	Atharvaveda Saṃhitā
BG	Bhagavad-Gītā
BGB	Bhagavad-Gītā-Bhāṣya
BS	Brahma-Sūtra
BSB	Brahma-Sūtra-Bhāṣya
BU	Bṛhadāraṇyakopaniṣad
CU	Chāndogyopaniṣad
GPK	Gauḍapādakārikā
ĪU	Īśopaniṣad
KU	Kaṭhopaniṣad
MāU	Māṇḍūkyopaniṣad
MB	Mahābhārata
MU	Muṇḍakopaniṣad
PU	Praśnopaniṣad
RV	Ṛg-veda Saṃhitā
ŚB	Śatapatha Brāhmaṇa
ŚU	Śvetāśvataropaniṣad
TU	Taittirīyopaniṣad
US	Upadeśasāhasrī
VC	Vivekacūḍāmaṇi
VP	Viṣṇu Purāṇa
YS	Yajurveda Saṃhitā

TABLE OF CONTENTS

CHAPTER I

INTRODUCTION

1. Puruṣa and Puruṣottama

In Indian Philosophical literature there has been always a search for the Ultimate Reality. Reality has been named as *Puruṣa*, *Ātman*, or *Brahman* in Indian tradition. *Puruṣa* and *Puruṣottama* are ambiguous terms.[1] A philosophical clarity of these terms is necessary as these ambiguous terms have led to much metaphysical speculations. I would like to find out their logical geography in my thesis. The ambiguous use of these terms in the *Prasthānatraya* has been elaborately discussed in the 2nd, 3rd and 4th chapters of my present work in the light of Śaṅkara's commentary. Here I would give a historical introduction to these two concepts as they developed in the Pre-Upaniṣadic Vedic period, and also how these terms featured in different Indian systems. The etymological meaning of the word *Puruṣa* is difficult to be conveyed. However, one can know the meaning by their uses in historical literature. In the *Saṁhitās*, the term *Puruṣa* has been used in the sense of the Ultimate Principle. "Who has seen the primeval (being) at the time of his being born, as the boneless one bears one that has no bones ?"[2] The Vedas designate this principle by various terms, viz., *Viśvakarman*, *Bṛhaspati*, *Prajāpati*, *Hiraṇyagarbha*,

1. S. Radhakrishnan, *Indian Philosophy*, Vol. 2., George Allen & Unwin Ltd., Ruskin House, 40 Museum St. W.C.I, 1958, p. 25.

2. Baldev Raj Sharma, *The Concept of Ātman in the Principal Upaniṣads*, Dinesh Publications, New Delhi, 1972, p. 15.

Jīva, *Suparṇa*, *Haṁsa*, *Puruṣa*, *etc.* "*Puruṣa* is verily all this (visible and invisible world), all that is and all that is to be, he is also the lord of immortality; for he mounts beyond (his own condition) for the food of the living being."[3] He is the one Reality, all-pervading, is manifested in different names and forms. The Whole Universe is non-different from Him.

> This Reality exists by itself. It is not subject to physical causal laws. All laws arise from it but the Reality is not the effect of any cause; instead, it is the cause and source of all effects. As a cause, it is earlier than all gods, who are far removed from it.[4]

In the *PS* (*RV* X.82.6), there is a detail discussion of the concept *Puruṣa*, the cause of the Universe. It is the material as well as the efficient cause of the Universe. One fourth of it is *Virāj*, the manifested world, and three fourths remain beyond the Universe in secrecy *(guhāyām)*. The world with all its evolutes is the product of this *Puruṣa* which is the cause of the movable and immovable objects of the world. Thus, the Vedic *Puruṣa* is the cause of all—'the begetter as well as the begotten', writes S. Radhakrishnan. He is the Ultimate Cause and He has no further cause of His own, looks after 'the order of the Universe', the *Ṛta*. The *Ṛta* is the unchanging Reality, 'the controlling spirit' which exists before the creation. In other words, It is the First Cause, the Uncaused Cause of the whole world. "*Puruṣa* is all this world, what has been and shall be" (*RV* X. 90.2). The *PS* further adds :

> The *Puruṣa* having occupied the whole Universe exceeded it by ten *aṅgulas*. This *Puruṣa* is the limit *(Kāṣṭhā)*, this *Puruṣa* is the goal, beyond which there is no goal (*Parāgatiḥ*) Therefore, the one and the only, having attained and realiz-ed which, there is no return *i.e. Anāvṛtti*.[5]

The *Bhagavadgītā* and the *Upaniṣad* also support this view. The *BU* writes that *Puruṣa* is Brahman. He is all knowledge... .

3 Baldev Raj Sharma, *The Concept of Ātman in the Principal Upaniṣads*, Dinesh Publications, New Delhi, 1972.

4 *Ibid.*, p. 40.

5 S.G. Mudgal, *Advaita of Śaṅkara—A Reappraisal*, Motilal Banarsi-dass, Delhi, 1975, pp. 57-58.

He is the highest goal of life (III. ix. 28). The *Gītā* says, "*yaṁ prāpya na nivartante taddhāma paramaṁ mama*"(VIII.21). Having attained Him, there is no return for He is the goal.

In the *YV*, *Prajāpati* is taken as an All-Pervasive Ultimate Power. It is the material as well as the efficient cause of the sentient and insentient categories of the world.[6]

> The *Paramaṁ Guhā*, the greatest Secret, the final source of everything, does not manifest itself fully but only one quarter of it is manifested in the form of the universe and the remaining three (*AV* II.1.2) are the extremely secret quarters as described in the Ṛgvedic *Puruṣa-Sūkta*.[7]

The *AV* defines the term *Puruṣa* as "*Puraṁ yo brahmaṇo veda yasyāḥ puruṣa ucyate*" (*AV* X.2.28). "It being created up, it being created crosswise, the *Puruṣa* pervaded in all the directions, who knows Brahman's city (*puram* or body) from which (He) is called *Puruṣa*."[8]

The evolution of the concept *Puruṣa* could be found in the *Upaniṣads* also. The *KU* holds the view that *Puruṣa* or Spirit is the ultimate principle of the world (I.3.11). The Vedic *Puruṣa* is taken up by *Upaniṣads* and developed further. '*Puriśaya iti Puruṣaḥ*'. The *Puruṣa* is so called because it resides in all the bodies *(puras)* as a citizen *(puriśaya puruṣa)*. The *BU* defines the term *puruṣa* as '*puriśaya iti Puruṣaḥ*' that is 'inhabiting the citadal of heart'. *Puruṣa* in the *Upaniṣads* is 'self-luminous' or self-sufficient. The self-luminousity of *Puruṣa* is established in the *BU* by an elaborate examination of the waking and dream consciousness—'*Atrāyaṁ Puruṣaḥ svayaṁjyotir bhavati*' (IV.3.14). The *CU* says His form is light—*bhā-rūpaḥ* (III.14.2) *Puruṣa* is described in the *Upaniṣads* as *hṛdyantar jyotiḥ*—the light of the heart (*BU*.I.3.7). In the *Upaniṣads*, the Ultimate Reality is sometimes viewed under the triple aspects of Brahman, Ātman, and the world, though no distinction between them in fact is intended.[9]

6 Baldev Raj Sharma, *The Concept of Ātman in the Principal Upaniṣads*, p. 74.

7 *Ibid.*, p. 76.

8 *Ibid.*, p. 78.

9 M. Hiriyana, *Outlines of Indian Philosophy*, George Allen and Unwin Ltd., London, 1973. p. 132.

There is the triple *Puruṣas* of the *Gītā* also, viz., the *Kṣara*, the *Ākṣara* and the *Puruṣottama*. The *Kṣara* is taken as the Changing Universe *(sarva bhūtātman)*, the *akṣara* as the *kūṭasthamāyā-śakti* of the Lord and the *Puruṣottama* as the Supreme Spirit. The Supreme Spirit is viewed either as the Impersonal Upanisadic Absolute or a Personal Lord of the *Gītā*. In fact, there is no distinction between the personal and the impersonal Spirit, the God of the Religion and the Absolute of the Philosophy. "This same Universal Spirit, which from one point of view may be regarded as God and from another point of view as the Absolute, takes on both personal and impersonal shapes, inasmuch as it essentially transcends them both."[10] Thus, the Upanisadic Absolute had to appear as a personal God of the *Gītā* which could act as 'the friend, philosopher and guide' of the mankind.[11] The Upaniṣadic Brahman is both cosmic and acosmic. From the cosmic standpoint, Brahman is taken as *saguṅa*. It is the cause of the world. Causal chain at best can be extended to the level of Cosmic Absolute *(*i.e. *Īśvara)*. The Absolute which is acosmic is beyond the causal chain, beyond all relations *(asparśa)*. It is non-conceptual. It is the state of Pure Consciousness. It is *Akṣara* of the *Prasthānatraya*. The *taṭastha-lakṣaṇa* of Brahman invests Brahman with attributes. The Upanisadic statements like "The Source from which the world proceeds, by which it is maintained or ended", or "That from which these beings are born, that, by which, when born they live, that into which, when departing, they enter. That, seek to know, That is Brahman" (*TU* III.1.1) give the *taṭastha-lakṣaṇa*, the non-essential, the accidental characteristics of Brahman. This is also the same as God or *Īśvara*. These are the *lakṣaṇas* of a conditioned Brahman. The conditioned Brahman is the *abhinnanimittopādānakāraṇa* of the world. Thus, the *saguṇa* Brahman of the *Upaniṣads* is the *Īśvara* or *Puruṣottama*

10 S.K. Belvalkar and R.D. Ranade., *History of Indian Philosophies—The creative period*, Oriental Book Reprint Corporation, New Delhi, 1955, p. 266.

11 M.K.V. Iyer, *Advaita Vedānta*, Asian Publishing House, New York, 1964, p. 14.

of the *Gītā*, which is the creator, maintainer and destroyer of *prapañca*, caught in the meshes of *māyā*, conditioned and limited. God is the *karmādhyakṣa*. He is *māyā-viśiṣṭa caitanya*. But he is not affected by *māyā*. *Māyā* is within His control. The Personal God of the *Gītā* is celebrated as the Supreme Person *(Puruṣottama)* in the world and in the *Veda*: '*Ato'smi loke Vede ca prathitaḥ Puruṣottamaḥ*' (*BG* XV.18). "It is not, therefore, merely a popular view, or an opinion of the world" writes Mr. Mudgal, "but the conclusion of the *Vedas* and is true of the released also, e.g., *Utāmṛtatvasyeśānaḥ (RV, PS)* or *Paramajyotīrūpa sampadya...as Uttamaḥ Puruṣaḥ. Puruṣottamamātrajñāna* is thus *śāstradṛṣṭi* too, as much as it is *lokadṛṣṭi*. The Supreme *Puruṣa* is hinted at in the *BU* who is 'the highest goal, surpassing all the eight *Puruṣas*, the *Devas*, the *Lokas* and their seats, though present in them, yet trancends them, controls them, governs them as their indweller"[12] The *ŚU* supports this view—"There is no other single God, who is hidden in all beings, who pervades all, who is the inner soul of all *(sarvasya cāhaṁ hṛdi sanniviṣṭaḥ)*" (VI. 11). It further adds —"Beyond this there is nothing Supreme... ."[13] The *TU* and the *MU* also advocate the sovereignty of the lord over the world of sentient and non-sentient beings (*TU* III.i.1, II.i.1, *MU* I.i.7, II.i.8).[14]

Śaṅkara writes that Ātman in the *MāU* does refer to *Antaryāmi* Brahman—the inner controller in all states. "Antar-yāmin is referred to *Sthūlabhuk* (in waking state), *Praviviktabhuk* (in dream), and *Ānandamaya* (in deep sleep state). The *Gītā* and the *Upaniṣads*, speak of the *Antaryāmin* Brahman as *bhoktā*, the enjoyer, etc. *(Ahaṁ hi sarvayajñānāṁ bhoktā ca prabhureva ca)* (*BG* IX.24 and *KU* I.3.1). He is the Supreme *Puruṣa* who resides in the heart (*hṛdi antarjyotiḥ puruṣaḥ*). The *Śruti* describes this *Puruṣa* in very many ways. "He is omniscient *(sarvajña)*, all-powerful *(sarvaśaktisamanvitam)*, the cause of the world

12 S.G. Mudgal, *Advaita of Śaṅkara : A Reappraisal*, Motilal Banarsidass, Delhi, 1975, p. 57.

13 *Ibid.*, p. 58.

14 *Ibid.*, p. 58.

(*ṣvarūpakāraṇaviṣayāṇi—BS* I.1.2); eternally Pure (*nitya śuddha —BS* I.1.2), above all evil (*CU* I.6.7). He is immanent Principle (*antaryāmin*), which fills the whole world and is the Soul, the Controller, the Immortal (*BU* III.7.22). He is the eternal, all-pervading cause of the world (*BS* II.1.24).[15] In the *US* (10.8) it is said :

> Though I am the Lord always the same in all beings, beyond the perishable and the imperishable, and therefore the Supreme, the Self of all, and without a second, I am considered to be of a contrary nature on account of Ignorance.[16]

Īśvara and Brahman are the intuitional and intellectual ways of apprehending the same Reality.[17] Brahman becomes *Īśvara* by means of *māyā*. *Īśvara* is the link between man and the Absolute. "Beyond *Īśvara* lies the Pure Being, devoid of the subject-object dualism which, after all, is the source and support of a successful *sādhanā*."[18]

The *Prasthānatraya* discusses both *Īśvara* and Brahman as the same object related to two ways of worship. "United with his creative power, *Puruṣottama* is Supreme and in his state of Pure Being, He is Brahman."[19] The Upaniṣadic *sūtrakāras* find no distinction between *Īśvara* and Brahman. "The Vedic conception of Reality as *tad-ekam* ... that one is sought to be replaced in the *Upaniṣads* by the absolute unity of '*ekam eva advitīyam*'... only the one, without the other."[20]

The Cārvākas rejected this Highest Reality altogether. They considered the body qualified with consciousness to be the

15 D. Prithipal, *Advaita Vedānta*, Bhāratīya Vidyā Prakāśan, Varanasi, 1969.

16 Swami Jagadananda, *A thousand Teachings of Śrī Śaṅkarāchārya*, Sri Ramakrishna Math, Mylapore, Madras, 1949 p. 113.

17 Ruth Reyan, *Introduction to Indian Philosophy*, Tata Mac Graw Hill Publishing Co. Ltd., Delhi, p. 45

18 D. Prithipal, *Advaita Vedānta*, p. 41.

19 S.P. Atreya, "The Philosophy of Bhagavadgītā", *Darshan International*, Vol. XVII., No. 1., Jan. 1971, p. 69.

20 Balbir Singh, *The Conceptual Framework of Indian Philosophy*, Macmillan Company of India Ltd., 1976, p. 24.

Ultimate Reality[21].. '*caitanyaviśiṣṭaḥ kāyaḥ puruṣaḥ*'. The Jainas say, everything is produced from matter *(pudgala)*... '*Pūrayanti galanti ca pudgala*'. The Buddhists take this world as soul. For Jainas, it is matter. It is the very basis of the world. It is *mūrta* or material. It is *Puruṣa* for the Jainas. The Jainas like the Cārvākas refute the belief in a God, yet they accept the *arhats*, the Supreme Lords. "Every soul when it reaches its highest perfection becomes a *Paramātman* or Supreme Soul."[22] Reality is change for Buddha. Buddha is the Supreme God *(devādi-deva)* for the Hīnayānists. The Śūnyavādins say, all worldly things are unreal. The Absolute is the Ultimate Reality. The nature of this reality is beyond language and description. "Reality is *bhūtatathatā* or the essence of existence."[23] This corresponds to the *akṣara*$_1$ of the *Prasthānatraya*. The Vijñāna-vādins denied the reality of the external world and the existence of the Self. It is individualized momentary *Vijñāna*. The Mādhyamikas assert that Gautama Buddha was an incarnation of *Ādi-Buddha* or the Ultimate. The conception of Buddha as *Bhagavān* corresponds to that of *Īśvara* in the Vedānta.[24] He incarnates in this world to save all beings from sorrows and sufferings. There is no God. Man himself is his own God. One must realize it by becoming an *arhat*.[25]

The Vaiśeṣikas do not accept the Highest Reality. Nowhere do we find a reference to *Īśvara*. Although Kaṇāda accepts the authority of the *Vedas*, he bluntly denies the role of *Īśvara* in it. Praśastapāda says that creation and dissolution are caused by the will of the Lord.[26] Gautama makes a casual reference to *Īśvara*. *Īśvara* is the cause because it is seen that *karma* of man remains

21 C. D. Sharma, *A Critical Survey of Indian Philosophy*, Motilal Banarsidass, 1964, p. 42.

22 S. Radhakrishnan, *Indian Philosophy*, Vol. I., George Allan & Unwin Ltd., 1948, p. 592.

23 C.D. Sharma, *op. cit.*, p. 121.

24 Balbir Singh, *The Conceptual Framework of Indian Philosophy*, Macmillan Company of India Ltd., 1976, p. 65.

25 *Ibid.*, p. 66.

26 C. Bulcke, S.J., *The Theism of Nyāya-Vaiśeṣika*, Motilal Banarsidass, 1968, p. 25,

fruitless (*Īśvaraḥ kāranaṁ puruṣa-karmāphalya-darśanāt—Nyāyasūtra* IV. 1.19).[27] Similarly, Vātsyāyana emphasises that God can't be conceived otherwise. God is a distinct soul endowed with certain qualities as a being of the same kind as soul, he can't be put under any other category (*guṇa-viśiṣṭam ātmāntaram īśvaraḥ ; tasya ātmakalpāt kalpāntarānupapattiḥ*—Vātsyāyana on *Nyāyasūtra* IV.1.21).[28] God is the *karmādhyakṣa*, the supreme judge of the moral quality of all human deeds and *karmaphaladātā* according to the Nyāya-Vaiśeṣikas. He is the efficient cause of the world. There is no creation in the true sense of the term. In Udayana's *Kusumāñjali*, we find the various arguments advanced in favour of the existence of God. But all these are the later developments of the Nyāya-Vaiśeṣika. Prof. Hiriyana remarks, "it is instructive to note that in all probability the belief neither in God nor in the *Vedas* was originally a part of the Nyāya-Vaiśeṣikas' teaching."[29]

The Sāṅkhya System does not accept any form of Godhead, personal or impersonal. *Puruṣa* is not the same as God for them. Īśvarakṛṣṇa has not taken into account the concept of *Īśvara* in his *Sāṅkhya Kārikā*. In the *ŚU*, we find the mention of this term in course of the discussion of the Sāṅkhya Philosophy. *Puruṣa* and *Prakṛti* are the different aspects of the *māyā-śakti*. Creation and dissolution are possible for Him. Pañcaśikha, the propounder of *Nirīśvara* Sāṅkhya does not accept *Puruṣottama*. Almost all the eminent propounders of the Sāṅkhya School like Vācaspati, Anirudha, etc., refute this concept. Vācaspati says, *Īśvara* is *āptakāma*. Why should he take interest in the creation of the world ? But Vijñānabhikṣu is in favour of this concept. Quoting from *Purāṇas* and *Smṛtis* he says that both *Puruṣa* and *Prakṛti* merge in *Īśvara*. The non-existence of this term can't be admitted from the fact that it cannot be proved. '*Īśvara-asiddheḥ*' is a mere bold assertion. The question of the Highest Reality is meaningless for the Sāṅkhyas.

The Yoga School on the other hand, accepts *Īśvara* which

27 C. Bulcke, S.J., *op. cit.*, p 29.
28 *Ibid.*, p. 26.
29 *Ibid.*, p. 27.

is a distinctly qualified *Puruṣa*. He is Omniscient and Omnipresent. He, being intelligent, is the cause of association and dissociation of *Prakṛti* and *Puruṣa*. *Prakṛti* is *Pariṇāminitya* and thus, it is *Kṣara* (perishable), whereas *Puruṣa* is *Kūṭasthanitya* and thus, it is *Akṣara* (imperishable). God of Yoga is a special kind of *Puruṣa (puruṣaviśeṣa Īśvaraḥ)*. He is not the creator, preserver or destroyer of this world. He does not reward or punish anybody. He is in no way connected with the bondage and the liberation of the *Puruṣas*.

Both Prabhākara and Kumārila reject the term *Puruṣa* or *Īśvara* altogether. Prabhākara holds that *apūrva* but not a personal God is the Ultimate Reality. Śaṅkara, criticising Prabhākara, says, *apūrva* is non-spiritual. It can't exercise its power unless it is associated with a personal agency. Thus, the Mīmāṃsakas do not require a God. There is no creation and dissolution. "Finite material products arise and perish, and yet the world as such, the universe as a whole, goes on moving, uncreated and unperishable."[30]

The Vedāntic concept of the Ultimate Reality can be taken as both *Saguṇa* and *Nirguṇa*. *Saguṇa* Brahman is called *Īśvara* or *Puruṣottama*. He is the efficient as well as the material cause of the world. He is the ideal Being *(Puruṣottama)* having all perfections *(Vibhūtis)*. "From the *Vyavahārikadṛṣṭi*, God as well as the world are real. But from the standpoint of *Pāramārthikasattā*, such a description is accidental. The Absolute is indescribable in its true essence *(svarūpa-lakṣaṇa)* and can't be the creator of anything."[31] He is the controller of both moral and physical aspects of the Universe. He is the *Puruṣottama*. But the Absolute, Śaṅkara writes, is beyond all these discourses. It can't be expressed in language. It is the state of silence, says Śaṅkara. It is the Abode *(adhiṣṭhāna)* of all the *Puruṣas*—both *Kṣara*, *Akṣara* and *Puruṣottama*. It is the Uncaused Cause, neither the cause nor the effect. It is *Akṣara* of the *Prasthānatraya* as opposed to the *Saguṇa* Brahman which is also sometimes taken

30 Baldev Rāj Sharma, *The Concept of Ātman in the Principal Upaniṣads*, Dinesh Publications, New Deihi, 1972, p. 260.

31 Balbir Singh, *The Conceptual Frame work of Indian Philosophy*, p. 74.

as *Akṣara*. The unmanifested *Prakṛti* is *akṣara* and the manifested universe is *kṣara* for Śaṅkara. Thus, it follows from the nature of the case that one aspect of the Reality is called *Īśvara (akṣara)* being conditioned by *Māyā*. *Māyā* is the adjunct of *Īśvara*. It is the First Cause of the world, writes Prof. Hiriyana. It corresponds to the *Prakṛti* of the Sāṅkhya-Yoga. The Vedāntins hold the view that the concept *Īśvara* or *Saguṇa* Brahman is meaningful only in the empirical discourse. Śaṅkara admits of a subtle body for *Īśvara*. He is the Lord of the empirical world of time, space and causation, writes Mr. Mudgal. But it can't be taken as the Ultimate of the Philosophy. The Ultimate of the Philosophy is beyond the moral and physical discourses. It is the state of *anirvacanīya*.

Rāmānuja on the other hand, quoting passages from the *Upaniṣads*,[32] *Gītā*[33] and *Purāṇas*[34] says that the Highest Reality is a qualified Brahman having many auspicious qualities. *Cit* (spirit) and *acit* (matter) are the body of God. '*Acit*' stands for *Kṣara*. It is the object Principle of all changes and modifications which are visible in the world.[35] '*Cit*' is taken as *Akṣara*. Both *cit* and *acit—akṣara* and *kṣara* are meaningful only from the standpoint of *Īśvara*.

Rāmānuja's God is both immutable and mutable—*akṣara* and *kṣara*. He is both the material and efficient cause of the

32 "*Dve vāva Brahmaṇo rūpe mūrtam caivāmūrtaṃ ca, martyam cāmṛtam ca yacca, sacca tyacca, athā nāmadheyam satyasya satyamiti.*" (*BU* II.3.1, 6).

33 "*Kṣarākṣarapuruṣābhyām avyayasvabhāvatayā vyāpanabharaṇaiśvaryādiyogena ca visajātīyam jānāti . . .*" (*BGB* 15.19). Rāmānuja's commentary on the *Gītā*, Gītā Press, Gorakhpur, samvat 2008, p. 14.

34 "The Highest Reality is called *Vāsudeva* in *VP*. He is the possessor of innumerable auspicious qualities. He is also free from all impurities." (Quoted from *A Critical Study of the Philosophy of Rāmānuja* by Anima Sengupta, Chowkhamba Sanskrit Series, Varanasi, 1967, p. 14).

Viṣṇu is designated as *saguṇa Īśvara* in *VP*. *The Pāñcarātra* literature accepts Lord *Viṣṇu* or *Vāsudeva* as the Highest Reality. He is omniscient, all perceiving and the sole support of the whole universe.

35 "*Acijjñānaśūnyam Vikārāspadam*",—*Tattvatraya*, Published by the Chowkhamba Sanskrit Series, Banaras, 1938, p. 34.

world. Rāmānuja takes *kṣara* for *Prakṛti*, *akṣara* for individual soul and regards *Puruṣottama* or the Supreme Self as superior to both these. Thus, "*Puruṣottama* is the concrete personality which is superior to the false abstructness of the infinite and finite", writes S. Radhakrishnan.[36] For Rāmānuja, *Nārāyaṇa* is the Highest Reality and is *Saguṇa* by nature. He is the *Puruṣottama* of the *Gītā*. *Prakṛti* and *Puruṣa* are its two nature. Rāmānuja finds no distinction between *Saguṇa* and *Nirguṇa* Brahman. He says, the Supreme Reality is one and it is both *Saguṇa* and *Nirguṇa*. For Rāmānuja, Brahman is *Saguṇa* in the sense He possesses all the auspicious qualities and He is also *nirguṇa* as He is devoid of all the inauspicious qualities. This brief historical survey shows how different systems' search for reality, is really a search for the meaning of *Puruṣa* and how this reality has been viewed at different times by the different systems.

I shall discuss in detail Śaṅkara's view on *Puruṣa* and *Puruṣottama* from my next Chapter.

2. *Scope of the Present Study*

The scope of the present study is confined to an enquiry into the concepts of *Puruṣa* and *Puruṣottama* and some similar concepts as found in Śaṅkara's commentary on the *Upaniṣad*, the *Brahma-Sūtra* and the *Gītā*. Śaṅkara's commentaries remain the most important works in Indian Philosophy even to-day. I propose to analyse critically these concepts, disentangle their different meanings and make an attempt to find out some of their implications in terms of Contemporary Philosophy in the light of Śaṅkara's commentary.

In what follows is set forth the main scheme of the present study. In Chapter II, I shall discuss the concept *Kṣara* as it is developed in the *Upaniṣads*, the *Brahma-Sūtra* and the *Gītā*. The key term is the *vyakta* in delineating the nature of the *kṣara puruṣa* in the *Upaniṣads*, whereas the *pradhāna* and the *bhūta* (*sarvabhūtānām*) are the key terms to understand the logical

36 S. Radhakrishnan, *Indian Philosophy*, Vol.1., George Allen & Unwin Ltd., 1948, p. 533.

geography of the *kṣara puruṣa* respectively in the *Brahma-Sūtra* and the *Gītā*.

Chapter III will embark upon a delineation of the various meanings of *Akṣara Puruṣa*. I shall take *Nirguṇa* Brahman as $akṣara_1$, *Māyā-śakti* as $akṣara_2$, *Praṇava* as $akṣara_3$ and *Īśvara* as $akṣara_4$.

In Chapter IV, I shall point out the nature of *Puruṣottama* as *Maheśvara* and *Daharākāśa* in the *Upaniṣads*. He is *Īśvara* in the *Brahma-Sūtra* and *Vāsudeva* in the *Gītā*.

Chapter V will discuss how the concepts of two Brahmans are fallacious and a criticism of 'the two-tier' and 'the double-decker' theory of Advaita Vedānta will be given. I shall also discuss the nature of causality and point out how Śaṅkara is a *satkāryavādin* so far as the phenomenal existence is concerned and how his *Vivartavāda* is not a theory of causality but a cancellation of it. I shall discuss the nature of *daharākāśa* and shall point out how Śaṅkara is not a mystic regarding his views on *dahara puruṣa*. A view that *Puruṣottama* is the ethically perfect man will also be discussed. Lastly, a number of logical characteristics of the *Puruṣottama* would be given.

CHAPTER II

KṢARA

1. *The Vyakta*

Usually one does not come across with the concept *Kṣara* in the *Upaniṣads*. The *ŚU* is perhaps the first *Upaniṣad* to use this concept in contrast to *Akṣara*.[1] In the *ŚU*, *Kṣara* is sometimes taken as *Pardhāna*,[2] sometimes as *Avidyā*,[3] and sometimes as *Vyakta*.[4] Whatever may be its import, *Kṣara* ordinarily means that which is perishable (*vināśaśīla*). The term is introduced in the *ŚU* wherein it is said :

> The Lord supports all this which is a combination of the mutable and the immutable, the manifest and the unmanifest. And the soul, not being the Lord, is bound because of his being an enjoyer. By knowing God (the soul) is freed from all fetters.[5]

Interpreting this *śloka*, Śaṅkara takes *Kṣara* as *Vyakta* or *Vikārasamūha* ... a conglomeration of manifested things. It is *vināśī* (perishable), whereas *Akṣara* is *Avyakta* and *Avināśī* (imperishable). Both *Kṣara* and *Akṣara* – the effect and the cause combined together from this world and

1 P. M. Modi, *Akṣara—A Forgotten Chapter in the History of Indian Philosophy*, Baroda State Press, Baroda, 1932, p. 139.

2 S. Radhakrishnan, *The Principal Upaniṣads*, George Allen and Unwin Ltd., London, 1953, p, 715.

3 *Ibid.*, p. 738,

4 *Ibid.*, p. 714.

5 *Ibid.*, p. 714.

the Lord maintains this.[6] Thus, in the cause-effect series the effects of the universe are to be traced back to that which is *Akṣara* or the root of the universe. But borh the *Kṣara* and the *Akṣara* ultimately depend on *Īśvara*. They form a triad. But beyond this causal triad, there is the Brahman. The 7th *śloka* of the *ŚU* which reads as follows :

> This has been sung as the supreme Brahman and in it is the triad. It is the firm support, the imperishable. The knowers of Brahman by knowing what is therein become merged in Brahman, intent thereon and freed from birth.[7]

This implies peculiarly that the *Akṣara* (immutable) also belongs to the category of *Kṣara* (mutable) fr om the standpoint of *Īśvara*. The *Śvetāśvatara's* use of the term *Avyakta* for *Kṣara*, "*Vyaktaṁ Kṣaraṁ Vināśya*" and *Avyakta* for *Akṣara* is also found in the *Gītā*.[8]

Śaṅkara writes that the *Paramātman* upholds this universe which consists of both the *Vyakta* (*Kṣara*) and *Avyakta* (*Akṣara*). Śaṅkara makes it further clear that the *ajā-Prakṛti* is united with the object of enjoyment (*bhogya*) and with the *bhoktā* (*Jīva*), "*Bhoktṛbhogyārthayuktā*."[9] The object of enjoyment (*bhogya*) here stands for the Mutable (*Kṣara*) and hence the *ajā-Prakṛti* can be designated as the *Kṣara*. In other words, *Kṣara* is called as *Pradhāna* (Primary Matter)[10] (*ŚU* I.10). Śaṅkara takes *Kṣara* as *Pradhāna* which is *Vināśaśīla* (perishable) and *amṛtākṣara* as *haraḥ*. The *Paramātman* (*Saccidānanda*) rules over these *Kṣara* and *ātmā*—the *Pradhāna* and *Puruṣa*.[11] This passage of the *ŚU* has a striking resemblance with

6 *Śaṅkarabhāṣya, ŚU*, Gītā Press, Gorakhpur, samvat 2016, p. 107 : "*Vyaktam Vikārajātamavyaktam Kāraṇam tadubhayaṃ Kṣaram Akṣaram ca Vyaktam Kṣaram Vināśyavyaktam Akṣaram Avināśī tadubhayam parasparasaṃyuktam kāryakāraṇātmakam Viśvam bharate Vibhatsa Īśvaraḥ.*"

7 S. Radhakrishnan, *The Principal Upaniṣads*, p. 714.

8 A. Mahādeva Śāstrī, *The BGB*, V. Rāmaswāmy Śāstrūlū & Sons, Madras, 1947, pp. 231-33.

9 *Śaṅkarabhāṣya, ŚU*, Gītā Press, Gorakhpur, samvat 2016. p. 113.

10 *Ibid.*, p. 119.

11 *Ibid.*, p. 119. : "*Sa Īśvaraḥ kṣarātmānau pradhāna-puruṣāviśata iṣṭedeva ekaścit sacchidānandādvitīyaḥ paramātmā*".

the 18th *śloka* of the 15th chapter of the *Gītā* wherein it is said that over the *Kṣara* and the *Akṣara*, one God (*Uttamaḥ Puruṣaḥ*) rules.

From the 12th *śloka* of the same *Upaniṣad* it is again understood that the term *Kṣara* is taken as the Primary Matter (*Pradhāna*). The threefold Brahman is being discussed '*bhoktṛ-bhoga-bhogya-rūpam*' here as (1) the enjoyer (*Jīva*), (2) the object of enjoyment (*Prakṛti*), and(3) the ruler (*devātma-śakti*).[12] This object of enjoyment (*Prakṛti*) is *bhogya* and hence, it is perishable (*Kṣara*). Thus, this *Prakṛti* (Nature) is *māyā* (illusion) and the Mighty-Lord (*Maheśvara*) is the illusion-maker (*māyin*)[13] who acts through this *māyā-śakti* or *devātma-śakti*. In the 8th *śloka* of the First *Adhyāya* of the same *Upaniṣad*, Śaṅkara makes it further clear that *kṣara* is *vyakta* or perishable (*vināśī*) and *avyakta* is *akṣara* which is imperishable (*avināśī*). This *avyakta* is the cause(*kāraṇa*) and the *vyakta* (*kṣara*) is its effect.[14] Thus the *Pradhāna* which is *kṣara* is the effect of the Immutable (*avyakta*). It is called *Avidyā*[15] (*ŚU* V. 1). The *ŚU* takes both *Pradhāna* and *Vyakta* as *Kṣara* (Mutable). Śaṅkara has used the term *Avidyā* as the "Knowledge of many detached from the one" and the "Knowledge of one is *Vidyā*". Hence, *Ayidyā* is *Kṣara* and *Vidyā* is *Akṣara* for Śaṅkara.

> In the imperishable, infinite highest Brahman are the two, knowledge and ignorance, placed hidden. Ignorance is perishable while knowledge is immortal. And he who controls knowledge and ignorance is another (distinct from either).[16]

Śaṅkara understands here the term *Kṣara* (*avidyā*) as the cause of the bondage and *vidyā* as the cause of *mokṣa* (*mokṣa-hetuḥ*)—'*kṣaraṁ tvavidyā kṣaraṇahetuḥ saṁsṛtikāraṇaṁ.*'[17] The Lord (*Īśa*) rules these two. He is the ruler of Primary Matter (*Pradhāna*)...'*Pradhānam avyaktam*' and of the spirit (*Kṣet-*

12 S. Radhakriṣhnan, *The Principal Upaniṣads*, George Allen & Unwin Ltd., London, 1953, p. 715.

13 *Śaṅkarabhāṣya*, *ŚU*, p. 197.

14 *Ibid.*, p. 107.

15 *Ibid.*, p. 215.

16 S. Radhakrishnan, *The Principal Upaniṣads*, p. 738.

17 *Śaṅkarabhāṣya*, *ŚU*, p. 216.

rajña)...'*kṣetrajño vijñānātmā*' and the Lord of the qualities, etc.[18] Again the term '*dve akṣara*' implies the idea of two imperishables (*akṣaras*)—the Immutable and the Mutable which is like the two unmanifests (*avyaktas*) of the *Gītā* (VIII. 20).[19] According to the *Gītā*, all beings (called the Mutable) rise from the lower unmanifest just as the Mutable in the form of 'not-knowledge' is to be traced to the Imperishable according to this verse of the *ŚU*.[20] Similarly, we come across a passage in the *KU* which reads :

> Abiding in the midst of ignorance, wise in their own esteem thinking themselves to be learned, fools treading a tortuous path go about like blind men led by one who is himself blind.[21]

Avidyā is the cause of bondage. One who lives in the midst of ignorance—'*avidyāyām antare*' suffers in this world. The *ĪU* supports this view by pointing out that one who worship the Unmanifest *Prakṛti* and *Avidyā* (ignorance) which is the seed of desire and work enter into blinding darkness.[22] Śaṅkara writes that *Avidyā* is equated with *Kṣara*. '*Vidyāṁ cāvidyāṁ ca devatājñānaṁ karma cety arthaḥ*.' It is *aparā-vidyā* (lower knowledge) dealing with things perishable, whereas *Vidyā* is *Parā-vidyā*.[23] The lower knowledge (*aparā-vidyā*) is called *Pradhāna* which is same as *Kṣara* and *Vyakta*.

The concept *Kṣara* is an ambiguous one as used in the *Upaniṣads*. It means that which is manifested whereas *Akṣara* means the cause of all the manifestations. But in the *ŚU* there is a *śloka* which says "the Supreme Brahman upholds both the enjoyer, the enjoyed and the Lord who maintains the two. Thus the *Paramātman* is different from the 'triad' (*trayam*), consisting

18 *Śaṅkarabhāṣya*, *ŚU*, p. 250.

19 P. M. Modi, *Akṣara—A Forgotten Chapter in the History of Indian Philosophy*, Baroda State Press, Baroda, 1932, p. 138.

20 *Ibid.*

21 Radhakriṣhnan, *The Principal Upaniṣads*, p. 609.

22 Swami Gambhirananda, *Eight Upaniṣads*, Vol. I, Advaita Ashrama, Calcutta-14, 1972, p. 20.

23 S. Radhakrishnan, *The Principal Upaniṣads*, George Allen & Unwin Ltd., London, 1953, p. 671.

of the individual soul, the world and the cosmic Lord."[24] In this sense, *Kṣara* concept would include both the manifest, the unmanifest and *Īśvara* also. Śaṅkara takes the *Īśvara* to be "Brahman reflected in *Māyā*."[25] And *Māyā* is *Kṣara*. In *PU* commenting on the 5th *śloka* of the second chapter, Śaṅkara understands by *sad-asat* as the formed and unformed—'*sat*—*mūrtam*', '*asata-amūrtam*'. Thus, *Akṣara* corresponds to *asat* and *Kṣara* corresponds to *sat*. In the *BU*, it is stated '*Dve vāva Brahmaṇo rūpe mūrtaṁ caiva amūrtaṁ ca, martyaṁ ca amṛtaṁ ca sthitaṁ ca yat ca sat ca tyat ca*'

> Two indeed are the forms of Brahman, that which is *Mūrta* and that which is *Amūrta* : the mortal and the immortal, the finite and the infinite, the decaying and the undecaying.[26]

In the *BU* again one finds a passage :

> For where there is duality as it were, there one smells another, there one sees another, there one hears another, there one speaks to another, there one thinks of another, there one understands another. Where, verily, everything has become the Self, then by what and whom should one smell, then by what and whom should one see, then by what and whom should one speak, then by what and whom should one think, then by what and whom should one understand ? By what should one know that by which all this is known ? By what, my dear, should one know the knower ?[27]

Thus, looked at from Brahman standpoint, *Īśvara*, *Jīva* and the world—all should be included in *Kṣara* as there is a duality in all of them. Looked at from the standpoint of *Īśvara*, the *Kṣara* would consist of the *Jīvas*, and the world as they are relatively less permanent. In another sense, *Kṣara* consists of all that is manifested, all that is concrete (*mūrta*), all that is *Vyakta* (individual).

24 S. Radhakrishnan, *The Principal Upaniṣads*, George Allen & Unwin Ltd., London, 1953, p. 714.

25 C.D. Sharma, *A Critical Survey of Indian Philosophy*, Motilal Banarsidass, Delhi, 1964, p. 385.

26 S.G. Mudgal, *Advaita of Śaṅkara—A Reappraisal*, Motilal Banarsidass, 1975, p. 67.

27 S. Radhakrishnan, *The Principal Upaniṣads*, p. 209.

2. *The Pradhāna*

As it has been pointed out before, the *Upaniṣad* takes this concept as opposed to the *Akṣara*. In the *Upaniṣads* the *Kṣara* is taken as *Pradhāna* (*Kṣara Pradhānam*), *avidyā* and *vyakta*. *Kṣara* stands for the manifested things which are perishable. The perishable is that which is liable to destruction. Hence, the point is raised; how can that which is perishable and that which is liable to destruction be the cause of anything ? The *Sūtrakāra* criticises the Sāṅkhya thinkers because for them the *Pradhāna* is the cause of the manifested Universe. *Pradhāna* (Primary Matter), being an object of enjoyment is *bhogya* and thus it is perishable. It is *Vyakta* (the manifest) as well as *Avidyā* (non-knowledge) for Śaṅkara. Śaṅkara writes that this Primary Matter being insentient can't be the cause of this Universe. The Sāṅkhyas argue that the *Pradhāna*, though insentient is omniscient because of its *sattva guṇa* and it is the material cause of the world being composite in nature.[28] To this the *Sūtrakāra* replies :

> The *Pradhāna* of the Sāṅkhya is not the cause of the Universe, because it is not mentioned in the *Upaniṣads*, which fact is clear from the fact of seeing (or thinking).[29]

Pradhāna has no power of seeing, to illumine, as it is insentient. Whenever it possesses that quality it is due to the omniscient Brahman says Śaṅkara. The Sāṅkhyas argue further, seeing is ascribed to the insentient *Prıdhānı* in a secondary sense just as in the cases of water and fire. "That fire saw" (*CU* VI.ii.3), "These waters saw" (*CU* VI.ii.4). But seeing can't be ascribed to *Pradhāna* because of the word 'self' says the Vedāntin.[30] The insentient *Pradhāna* do not have a sentient soul. "*Pradhāna* is not the meaning of the word 'self', because liberation is promised for one who holds on to That.[31] Liberation is meant for a sentient self but not for the un-Vedic

28 Swami Gambhirananda, *Brahma-Sūtra Bhāṣya of Śaṅkarācārya*, Advaita Ashrama, Calcutta, 1972, p. 46.

29 *Ibid.*, p. 47.

30 *Ibid.*, p. 52.

31 *Ibid.*, p. 54.

Pradhāna which is insentient. All sentient beings merge in a conscious entity, called 'Existence' which is the cause of the Universe. But *Pradhāna* is not so.[32] In all the *Upaniṣads* it is stated that consciousness is the cause. The omniscient and omnipotent God (Blissful One) is the cause of this world but not the *Pradhāna*.[33] Here, the term 'Blissful' does not stand either for *Pradhāna*, or for the individual self. It is the Supreme Self which is the Internal Ruler (*BU* I.ii.18). "Because the qualities that do not belong to *Pradhāna* are spoken of."[34] The individual self is subject to the limiting adjunct of the body and senses and hence, it can't be immutable. Here the term immutable means "the source of all things" (*MU* I.i.5).

> That by which is realised that immutable. Neither *Pradhāna* nor embodied soul can possibly be omniscient in general and all knowing in detail.[35]

Liberation can't be achieved by the *Pradhāna*. Thus it is said :

> God alone is the source of all things, and neither *Pradhāna* nor the individual soul is so[36] because of 'the distinctive characteristics'[37] and 'difference',[38] and 'the presentation of form.'[39]

The presentation of form such as "The indwelling self of all is surely He of whom heaven is the head, etc., can't be applicable to the embodied soul or to the *Pradhāna*."[40] All the presentations of forms like "*Puruṣa* is all this" (*MU* II.i.10) lead to the understanding of the Supreme Lord.[41] The Supreme

32 Swami Gambhirananda, *Brahma-Sūtra Bhāṣya of Śaṅkarācārya*, Advaita Ashrama, Calcutta, 1973, p. 60.

33 *Ibid.*, p. 65.

34 *Ibid.*, p. 135.

35 *Ibid.*, p. 139.

36 *Ibid.*, p. 142.

37 *Ibid.*, p. 143.

38 *Ibid.*, p. 143.

39 *Ibid.*, p. 144.

40 *Ibid.*, p. 144.

41 *Ibid.*, p. 145.

Lord is attained by the illumined soul even in this body (*BU* IV.iv.7). "But *Pradhāna* and the rest are nowhere known to be attainable by the liberated,"[42] says the Vedāntin. The *Sūtrakāra* further states :

> The act of supporting is possible for God only, owing to the mention of His mighty rule[43] and it is not possible in case of *Pradhāna*. The Sāṅkhya try to prove from the *smṛtis* and the *Upaniṣads*, etc. that the inferred entity *Pradhāna* is the cause.[44]

In *Kaṭhopaniṣad*, "The unmanifest (*Avyakta*) is higher than *mahat*, *Puruṣa* is higher than *avyakta* (I.iii.11), where *mahat*, *avyakta* and *Puruṣa* are found under the same epithets and in the same order as they are known from the Sāṅkhya *Smṛtis*. The word *avyakta* (*na vyakta*) stands for *Pradhāna* in Sāṅkhya *Smṛti*. It is being devoid of sound, etc. (*KU* I.3.15). The *avyakta* of the *KU* here does not refer to the *Pradhāna* as *Pradhāna* is taken as an independent cause comprising three attributes. It stands for body (in subtle form) *i.e.*, in the causal state but not for *Pradhāna*.[45]

> (*Avyakta* is not *Pradhāna*) because it is dependent on that (God), but this *avyakta* has to be admitted as it serves some purpose.[46]

Pradhāna is a thing to be known for the sake of acquiring supernatural powers.[47] But *avyakta* is not a thing to be known. Hence, *avyakta* does not refer to *Pradhāna*.[48] Śaṅkara interpretes *avyakta* not as the *Prakṛti* of the Sāṅkhya but 'the world fiction *Māyā* which is the body of *Īśvara* (*kāraṇa-śarīra*), the cosmic body out of which all things emanate'.[49] There is no Vedic sanction as such. Thus, in the *Upaniṣads*, it is the

42 Swami Gambhirananda, *Brahma-Sūtra Bhāṣya of Śaṅkarācārya*, Advaita Ashrama, Calcutta, p. 163.

43 *Ibid*., p. 176.

44 *Ibid*., p. 247.

45 *Ibid*., p. 248.

46 *Ibid*., p. 248.

47 *Ibid*., p. 252.

48 *Ibid*., p. 258.

49 A.E. Gough, *The Philosophy of the Upaniṣads*, Ess Ess Publications, Delhi, 1975, p. 201.

Supreme Self, but not *Pradhāna* which is mentioned, says the *Sūtrakāra*. Again, it is said :

> The word *ajā* does not refer to *Pradhāna*, because special characteristics have not been stated.[50]

Pradhāna can't explain the design of this Universe (*BS* II.ii.1). The external and corporeal things do have a cause and the insentient *Pradhāna* can't be taken to be the cause. The insentient things act under the guidance of a sentient being, viz., the potter (*BS* II.ii.2). The causal relationship holds good in case of Brahman or *Māyā*, says the Vedāntin.[51] Even the *Pradhāna* can't act spontaneously like milk and water for the good of the people (*BS* II.ii.3), because milk and water act under the guidance of some sentient beings.

> He who dwells in the water, yet is within the water, whom water does not know, whose body the water is, who controls the water from within, he is your self, the inner controller, the immortal.[52] Under the mighty rule of this Immutable, O Gārgī, some rivers flow eastward (*BU* III. vii. 9).

Thus, *Pradhāna* can't be taken to be the cause since nothing exists externally on which it can depend for either impelling or stopping.[53] It does not have any purpose of either experienee (of joy and sorrow) or liberation, or both. It does not act for the soul.[54] The passive soul can't impell *Pradhāna*,[55] which is devoid of intelligence.[56] Thus, from the above discussion it follows that *Pradhāna* which is *Kṣara* can't be the cause or the abode '*na anumānamatat Śabdāt*' (*BS* I. iii. 3). The *Pradhāna* being concrete in nature lacks creativity.

> Creativity presupposes potency and this is incapable of being found anywhere in the *Pradhāna*. Everything in it is a

50 Swami Gambhirananda, *Brahma-Sūtra Bhāṣya of Śaṇkarācārya*, Advaita Ashrama, Calcutta, 1972, p. 259.

51 *Ibid.*, p. 370.

52 S. Radhakrishnan, *The Principal Upanisads*, George Allen & Unwin Ltd, p. 226.

53 Swami Gambhirananda, *Brahma-Sūtra Bhāṣya of Śaṇkarācārya*, Advaita Ashrama, Calcutta, 1972, p. 374.

54 *Ibid.*, p. 376

55 *Ibid.*, p. 377.

56 *Ibid*,, p. 379.

product, an evolute. It can, therefore, be called an effect and never a cause in the ontological sense of the term.[57]

Thus, the *Sūtrakāra* takes a bold stand against the Sāṅkhyas on the ground that *Pradhāna*, which is concrete and finite, can't be the creative principle of the Universe.[58] That which creates the concrete and finite must be different from it and it must be infinite.

In the *SU* the term *Kṣara* is also taken as *avidyā* (not-knowledge) "*Kṣaraṁ tvāvidyā*," etc. In *BS*, we find the mention of this *avidyā* concept, "The Body and other things contained in the sphere of the Not-self are our eslf."[59] Or, The Body is the product of *Avidyā* (*BSB* I. iv. 4) or The Elemental substances and the sense organs are the products of *Avidyā* (I. iv. 22) or The Body and other limitative adjuncts are the products of *Avidyā* (II. iii. 48). It is the *aparā-vidyā* (lower knowledge) dealing with things perishable. This *aparā-vidyā* is called *Pradhāna* which is *kṣara* and *vyakta*.

3. *Sarva Bhūtāni*

The *BG* discusses the concept of triple *puruṣas* in its fifteenth chapter. In the same chapter, there is the description of a *Aśvattha* tree. This *Aśvattha* (*a* = not, *śva* = tomorrow, *tha* = not remaining tomorrow) means that which will no exist for tomorrow. In other words, it stands for that which is not permanent. The Universe is described here figuratively as a tree.[60] It is also called the cosmic Tree (*Jagat vṛkṣa*). *Saṁsāra* stands for the entire world, which can be seen by the eyes or 'the visible cosmos' which is known in Sāṅkya Philosophy as 'the diffusion of *Prakṛti*' and in Vedānta Philosophy, as the spreading out of the *Māyā* (Illusion) of the Blessed Lord. The 'diffusion of *Prakṛti*' forms the cosmic Tree

57 N.V. Joshi, *The Three Foutainheads of Indian Philosophy*, Somaiya Publictinos Pvt. Ltd., Bombay, 1972, p. 118.

58 Swami Gambhirananda, *Brahma-Sūtra Bhāsya*, p. 21. See also pp. 369-72.

59 *Ibid.*, p. 162.

60 A. Mahadeva Sastri, *The BGB*, V. Ramaswamy Sastrulu & Sons, Madras, 1947, p. 396.

according to Sāṅkhya Philosophy. The Vadāntins do not agree with this view. They say it is merely the branches of the *Ūrdhvamūla* (uprooted tree), *Pīppala* tree.[61] The *Gītā* makse an attempt to harmonise there two distinct views. This tree of *saṁsāra* extends its branches both below and above.

> Below and above its branches spread, nourished by the *guṇas*, sense objects its buds; and below in the world of man stretch forth the roots ending in action.[62]

Śaṅkara writes that right from man down the objects, unmovable, below and again from him upto the abode of *Brahmā*, the creator of this entire regions—stands for the spreading branches of that Tree. All beings (*bhūtas*) are nourished by the three categories of *guṇas* or qualities which form material support (*upādāna*) of all things and beings of this world. The nature of this material world is perishable (the *Kṣara*) like a tree. Thus the term *Kṣara*[63] is used in the *Gītā*

61 B.G. Tilak, *Śrīmad Bhagavad-Gītā Rahasya,* Lokamanya Tilak Mandir, Poona, 1903, p. 1138.

62 A. Mahadeva Śastri, *The BGB*, p. 399.

63 Śrī Rāmānuja would interprete the term *kṣara* as *baddhātmā* or unemancipated soul. He writes, "the *kṣara* consists of all beings that are associated with the non-intelligent *prakṛti* of a changeable nature, from *Brahmā* to a clump of grass who can be denoted by the expression, 'individual self' (*Jīva*)." Rāmānuja further defines, "the word *puruṣa* is used in the singular (as indicative of a class) by reason of the singular adventitious conditions of association with non-intelligent matter." —Quoted from Gitābhāṣya of Rāmānuja, tr. by M. R. Sampatkumar, Vidya Press, Madras, 1969, p. 432.

Tilak translates *kṣara* as all (perishable) beings, made up of the five primordial elements and the *akṣara* as the *kuṭastha* (homogeneous). Thus, both Śaṅkara and Tilak would agree that *kṣara* is *bhūta* or *Jaḍa-Padārtha.* Rāmānuja's concept of *kṣara* includes Tilak's both *kṣara* and *akṣara* as the subtle (*avyakta*) *prakṛti* is *akṣara* and *kṣara* is the visible cosmos for Tilak.

Śrī Madhva, unlike Rāmānuja, writes that *kṣara puruṣa* is the embodied soul. And Rāmānuja interpretes *kṣara* to be all sorts of entities which are connected with *prakṛti* . . ."*brahmādistambaparyanta-kṣaraṇasvabhāvācit-saṃsṛṣṭa-bhūtam*" (15.16).

The *kṣara puruṣa* undergoes modifications as it is subject to spatiotemporal existence. It is this cosmic existence, being subjective in nature enjoys the object of his consciousness. . ."*kṣaraḥ sarvāṇi bhūtāni*". Pt. Nilakantha in the sense of all beings *'sarva bhūtāni'*. While analysing critically the whole of *Gītā*, we find the term *Kṣara* being used directly in III.14-15, VII.4, VIII.18-19, XV.16, though thre is indirect reference of the same concept in many other passages. In the 16th stanza of the 15th Chapter of the *Gītā*, it is said :

Das interpretes the term *kṣara* as "*kṣareṣu, vikārvatsu, nāśaśīleṣu, vyakteṣu, bhūtamātreṣu, prabhavāprabhavādirūpeṇa vibhakta iva, avibhaktaḥ sthitaḥ.*" It is mutable, perishable, manifest, the conglomeration of the gross bodies.—Quoted from Pt. Nilakantha Das's *Śrīmad Bhagavadgītā*, New Students Store, Binodbihari, Cuttack, 1968, p. 384.

Interpreting the nature of the *kṣara* and *akṣara* of the *Gītā*, E.H. Johnston writes, "*kṣara* is equivalent to all beings, derives from *puruṣa* in its ordinary sense of 'man', and is the same as the *puruṣa* of the *PU* (IV. 9) and *sat puruṣa* of the *MU* (I. i. 7), the other is 'the *kṣara kūṭastha puruṣa*' that is the individual soul, the successor of the *akṣara-ātman* of the *PU* and the *ŚU*."—E.H. Johnston's. *Early Sāṇkhya*, Royal Asiatic Society, 1937, p. 75.

E. H. Johnston perhaps is not correct in taking 'the *kṣara kūṭastha puruṣa*' as the individual soul (or *jīvātman*) because, the term *kūṭa* means that which does not reveal the real nature of the things and *stha* means 'existence'. For Śaṅkara, *kūṭastha* means that which is unshakable. Thus it is imperishable and immutable and it stands for *akṣara puruṣa*. "When Śaṅkara and Śaṅkarite take *kṣara* as an evolutionary product, Mādhvites take it as finite souls and Viśvanātha Cakravartī says it is the finite differentiated consciousness." — Quoted from M. N. Sircar's *Hindu Mysticism*, Bharatiya Mahavidyalaya, Calcutta, 1943, pp. 82-85.

"In *AS* at 8764-7, the ātman is described as twofold, the *kṣara*, the corporeal being and *akṣara*, the soul. At 11434 of the same treatise it is said :

Tadā kṣaratvaṃ prakṛtir gacchate guṇasaṃśritaṃ.

Nirguṇatvaṃ ca Vaideha guṇeṣv aparivartanāt.

Again, at 11364, *kṣara* is described as *nānātva* as opposed to *akṣara* which is *ekatva*. According to Sāṅkhya Philosophy, *kṣara* is many. It is identified with *Pradhāna*, with its lower Nature and the *Akṣara* is one "*ekatvam akṣaram prāhur nānātvam kṣaram ucyate.*" (*MB* XII. 305-36 c-d). Thus, the *kṣara* represents the mutable, manifold, physical existence and the *akṣara* is unity, reality, true knowledge, unchangeableness."—Quoted from E. H. Johnston's *Early Sāṅkhya*, p. 77.

There are those two beings in the world, the perishable and the imperishable: the perishable comprises all creatures, immutable is called the imperishable.[64]

They are spoken as *Puruṣas*, because they are the *upādhis* of *Puruṣa*, the one Spirit, says Śaṅkara. Out of these two categories, one is called *Kṣara* and the other one as *Akṣara*. The *Kṣara* comprises the whole universe with the changing names and forms. Śaṅkara would like to point out that the whole of the *Aṣvattha* representing the collection of unconscious objects (*Jaḍa-padārtha*) stands for *Kṣara* or perishable. The synonyms of *Kṣara* are the *bhūtas* (mutable), *bhūtāni* (all beings), *adhibhūta* (the material form), the *kṣetra* or *śarīra* (physical body), the *vyakta* (manifest), the *aparā-Prakṛti* (lower Nature or non-mental), *avidyā* (not-knowledge), etc. The *BGB* reveals the true meaning of this concept in its manifold aspects.

Sacrifice is born of Action, know thou that action comes from Brahman, and that Brahman comes from the Imperishable. Therefore, the all-pervading Brahman ever rests in sacrifice.[65]

Śaṅkara would like to interprete that *Kṣara* consists of all beings and this *Kṣara* (lower Nature) is born out of the Highest Self of the Immutable. In the *Gītā*, we fiind the description of two natures—the lower and the higher of the same *Īśvara*. The higher nature is spirit (*kṣetrajña*) 'which substains the whole universe' and the lower is matter (*kṣetra*) from which all beings are born. The *ksetra* (*kṣara*) is the inferior *Prakṛti* (*aparā*) and the *kṣetrajña* or *jīva* is the superior *Prakṛti* (*parā*) of *Īśvara*. Śaṅkara understands the term superior *Prakṛti* (*parā*) as *kṣetrajña*, or individual self. '*Kṣetrajña*, *Jīva* and *Bhoktṛ* (enjoyer) are all synonymous terms for *Puruṣa*.' *Puruṣa* is the cause. It is a 'conditioned being.'[66]

When the *aparā-prakṛti* (*kṣara*) and the *parā-prakṛti* (individual self) unite together, they form the *Yoni* or the womb of all beings (*sarva bhūtāni*) (*BGB* VII. 6, p. 210). The *Yoni* of *Īśvara* for giving birth to all beings is *Mahad*

64 A Mahadeva Sastri., *The BGB*, V. Ramaswamy Sastrulu & Sons, Madras, 1947, pp. 409-10.
65 *Ibid.*, p. 100.
66 *Ibid.*, p. 209. also see pp. 317-18.

Brahma which is the combination of matter and spirit, *kṣara* and individual self.[67]

Both the *aparā* and *parā Prakṛti* constitute *Kṣara.* All beings are made up of these two.[68] The inferior Nature with its eightfold principles is the '*māyā* belonging to the *Īśvara*'[69] and the higher nature is *kṣetrajña* which sustains the whole world.

> Brahman is the Imperishable (*Akṣara*), the Supreme. The Ego is said to be the Individual Self (*Adhyātma*, He who dwells in the body). The offering which causes the origin of physical beings is called action (*Karma*).[70]

Karma is the seed of all beings. It is by the act of creation (*Visarga*) alone, all beings, both animate and inanimate are born. This physical region (*Adhibhūta*) is the perishable existence (*Kṣarabhāva*). Śaṅkara writes *Adhibhūta* as :

> That which gathers itself round the whole animated creation and is composed of the whole perishable existence, i.e., of everything that has birth (*adhibhūtaṁ kṣarobhāvaḥ*).[71]

This is the material or immanent from of the Lord. The *Gītā* describes this form of the Lord in VIII. 7-12, X. 20-42 and XV. 12-15 stanzas. The five elements viz., the space, the air, the fire, the water and the earth are designated as *adhibhūta* which is perishable. the *Adhibhuta* is the material in contrast to the *Adhyātma* which is spiritual.

> From the Unmanifested all the manifestations proceed at the coming on of a day; at the coming on of a night they dissolve there only, in what is called the Unmanifested.[72] This same multitude of beings having come into being again and again, is dissolved at the coming on of night, not of their will, and comes forth at the coming on of day.[73]

67 A. Mahadeva Sastri, *The BGB*, V. Ramaswamy Sastrulu & Sons Madras, 1947, pp. 380-381.

68 N.V. Joshi., *The Three Fountainheads of Indian Philosophy*, Somaiya Publications Pvt. Ltd., Bombay, 1972, p. 93.

69 A. Mahadeva Sastri, *The BGB*, p. 209.

70 *Ibid.*, p. 223.

71 A. Mahadeva Satri, *The BGB*, V. Ramaswamy Sastrulu & Sons, Madras, 1947, p. 224.

72 *Ibid.*, p. 231.

73 *Ibid.*, p. 232.

The lower unmanifest (*avyakta*) in the 18th *śloka*, which is called as *Avidyā* is the source of all beings, out of which all creatures (both *sthāvara* and *jaṅgama*) are manifested at the beginning of a day and all are dissolved at the end on of a night and this lower unmanifest is nothing but *Kṣara* or the Mutable existence. But 20th *śloka* of the same chapter describes the nature of another *avyakta* (*sanātana avyakta*) called *akṣara* which does not perish when all beings perish. All manifestations *Vyaktis* arise from the lower unmanifest which is distinct from the higher unmanifest called the *akṣara*.[74] Again, in *BG* II.28, II.30 the Lord advises Arjuna not to feel sorry for the death of the bodies since the nature of all being is mutable. All these beings are absorbed into the lower unmanifest which is composed of three *guṇas* at the end of a *Kalpa* and again these beings are created at the beginning of (the next) *Kalpa*.[75] In the 7th chapter of the *Gītā* we find that there is the description of the nature of the Lord, as the *aparā-prakṛti* (*Kṣara*) and the *parā-Prakṛti* (*Jīva*). This *aparā-Prakṛti* is composed of three *guṇas* and it is eightfold in nature.

> It transforms itself into all objective forms, such as the bodies (*Kārya*), the sense (*Kāraṇa*) and the sense-objects (*Viṣaya*), and is combined into various aggregates of the body and the senses, to subserve the two ends of *Puruṣa* of Spirit, viz., enjoyment and liberation. Such an aggregate is this, body.[76]

In the 13th chapter of the *Gītā* (XIII.1, 3, 5, 6) the nature of the body (*Kṣetra*) has been discussed.

> This *Kṣetra*—the field, the body, matter—is so called because it is shielded from injury, or because it is destructible, or because it is liable to decay.[77]

The *Kṣetra* constitutes the five primordial elements and the rests and hence it is included in the *Kṣara*.[78] The *Kṣetra* is

74 A. Mahadeva Satri, *The BGB*, V. Ramaswamy Shstrulu & Sons. Mdras, 1947, p. 231.

75 *Ibid.*, p. 243.

76 *Ibid.*, pp. 316-17.

77 *Ibid.*, p. 317.

78 *Ibid.*, p. 337.

Jaḍa-padārtha (*savikāra*). And this *Jada-Padārtha* stands for *Kṣara* which undergoes modification. *Aparā-Prakṛti* is described in the *Gītā* as inferior one. It is *Jaḍa* (gross), dependent and is the cause of this *saṁsāra*. The *Jīva* falls in the bondage of *saṁsāra* because of this *aparā-Prakṛti*. All beings both movable and immovable are born out of the combination of *parā* and *aparā Prakṛti* which is relative and finite (*Kṣara*). But the Sāṅkhya thinkers make a sharp distinction between the *Kṣara* and the *Akṣara* to express the difference between the real and apparent existence. According to Sāṅkhya :

> The *Kṣara* is many. It is identified with *Pradhāna*, with its lower Nature and the *Akṣara* is one. Thus, the *Kṣara* represents the mutable, manifold physical existence.[79]

Avidyā (not knowledge) the opposite of knowledge (*Vidyā*) in the Mutable (*Kṣara*) and *Vidyā* is the Immutable *Akṣara* identified with the 'Immortal'. The *Upaniṣad* proclaims, '*Kṣaraṁ tu avidyā hy amṛtaṁ tu vidyā vidyāvidye.*' The *Gītā* takes the lower Nature (*Adhibhūta*) as the abode of *avidyā* and all beings rise from this.

Kṣara is designated as *Vyakta* (Manifest). It is also called *Pradhāna* (the lower Nature). The lower Nature constitutes the objects of enjoyments. Thu s, this term *Kṣara* has been use in different ways in the whole of the *Gītā*. Whatever may be its different interpretations, all would agree on the point that the term *Kṣara* which stands for mutability but not total destruction is one of the aspect of the same Reality as opposed to 'the *Akṣara*'. The reading of the *Gītā* distinctly points out that in this manifold universe, we experience the two *puruṣas*, the *Kṣara* and the *Akṣara*, which is '*avyakta akṣara*' or '*kuṭastha*'. The *Kṣara Puruṣa* being associated with the lower Nature (*Prakṛti*) appears to be the doer of all actions (*Kartā*). But this is not the final stage of learning. To know the Reality as the *Kṣara* only is to know it half hazardly. The *Aśvattha*, the tree of *Saṁsāra* comprises both the *Kṣara* and the *Akṣara*. To conceive it as *Kṣara* only is not to know its root. *Kṣara* and *Akṣara* are thus

79 E. H. Johnston, *Early Sāṅkhya*, Royal Asiatic Society, London, 1937. p. 77.

relative terms. *Kṣara* means mutable or changing and its import would be derived from that which is immutable or unchanging.

Śaṅkara would take a hierarchy of changing orders. The world of the manifestations are changing or *Kṣara* and in comparison with it the *Kuṭastha-Prakṛti* is *Akṣara*. In every *Kalpa*, manifestations come out of it. But *Kuṭastha-Prakṛti* can be taken as a part of the *Kṣara* when it is viewed from the standpoint of *Īśvara*. But that which never changes, which sustains all these three—*Īśvara*, *Kuṭastha-Prakṛti* or *Māyā* and the manifestations of *Māyā* is the Supreme Brahman. Thus, the concept of change necessarily brings in the concept of that which is not changing and in their relentless search for that which is unchanging, the *Prasthānatraya* went from *saṁsāra* to *māyā*, from *māyā* to *Īśvara* and then from *Īśvara* to Brahman. We propose to discuss the concept of *Akṣara* which is taken to be the root of *Kṣara* in our next chapter.

CHAPTER III

AKṢARA

1. *The Upaniṣads*

Like *Kṣara*, the *Akṣara* is also an ambiguous concept. Roughly speaking, the *Upaniṣads* use this term sometimes as the Brahman, sometimes as the *Jīvātman*, sometimes as *Parā-Prakṛti*, sometimes as *Adhyātma*, sometimes as the '*Kūṭastha-māyā-śakti*' and sometimes as the syllable *Om*. Unless one is sure about the meaning of the term and the context in which a particular meaning is used, one is likely to commit mistake. Hence, a terminological precision and clarity is necessary. Therefore, I would like here to make an attempt for a systematic study of this most confused term. To avoid confusion and misunderstanding it may be suggested to use $akṣara_1$ for the Brahman and $akṣara_2$ for the *Kūṭastha māyā* and $akṣara_3$ for he syllable *Om**, and ($akṣara_4$) for the *Īśvara*.

(A) *Nirguṇa* Brahman ($Akṣara_1$)

$Akṣara_1$ at the outset appears to be Brahman in almost all the major *Upaniṣads*. Brahman is the Immutable (*akṣara*). "This Brahman is neither gross, nor fine, neither short, nor long......"[1]

> Verily, O Gārgī at the command of that Imperishable, the sun and the moon stand in their respective positions.[2] Verily, O Gārgī, that Imperishable is unseen but is the

1 S. Radhakrishnan, *The Principal Upaniṣads*, George Allen and Unwin Ltd., London, 1953, p. 232.

2 *Ibid.*, p. 232.

Seer, the unheard but is the hearer, the unthought but is the thinker, unknown but is the knower.[3]

The *PU* discusses this by pointing out two types of Brahman, the superior and the inferior Brahman (*param ca aparam ca*).

Whosoever, O Gārgī, in this world, without knowing this Imperishable performs sacrifices, worships, performs austerities for a thousand years, his work will have an end.[4] The Superior Brahman is Immutable and is called *Puruṣa.* Words can't directly express this Brahman, which is free from all adjuncts.[5] It is further said that *vijñānātmā Puruṣa* (the *Jīva*) gets wholly established '*pare akṣara ātmani*' in the supreme immutable Self.[6]

He who realises that shadowless, bodiless, colourless, pure, Immutable attains the supreme Immutable Itself"[7] (*Param eva akṣaram*). This *akṣara*$_1$ is bodiless (*aśarīram*), colourless (*alohitam*) etc.

O amiable one, he becomes all knowing and enters into all who knows that Immutable wherein merges the cognising self (the *Puruṣa*, who is naturally a knower)—as also do the organs and the elements together with all the deities.[8]

The *MU* writes "then there is the higher (knowledge) by which is realised that Immutable (*akṣara*)."[9] (*Akṣaram adhigamyate*). "This higher knowledge stands for *akṣara*$_1$ which can't be experienced and grasped, which is without source, featureless, eyes and ears, which has neither hands, nor feet, which is eternal, multiformed, all pervasive, extremely subtle, and undiminishing and which is the source of all."[10]

Śaṅkara further makes it clear by pointing out that 'That

3 S. Radhakrishnan, *The Principal Upaniṣads*, 1953, p. 233.

4 *Ibid.*, p. 233.

5 Swami Gambhirananda, *Eight Upaniṣads*, Vol. II, Advaita Ashrama, Calcutta, 1972, p. 470.

6 *Ibid.*, p. 466.

7 *Ibid.*, pp. 466-67.

8 *Ibid.*, p. 468.

9 *Ibid.*, p. 87.

10 *Ibid.*, p. 89.

is the higher knowledge by which the Immutable of this kind is realised.[11] This *akṣara*$_1$ can be attained by one who approaches it as per the instructions of the scriptures, 'whose heart is calm and whose outer organs are under control.' The *akṣara-Puruṣa* or *akṣara*$_1$ is pure, transcendental, and devoid of all forms (*nāmarūpāt vimūktaḥ*)." "It is higher (*parataḥ akṣarāt*) as compared with the (other) higher immutable called the unmanifested (i.e., *Māyā*)."[12] Thus, this *akṣara*$_1$ of the *Upaniṣads* is the Vedāntic '*paramam brahman*' (Supreme Brahman). "Any one who knows this becomes Brahman indeed."[13] It is 'the supreme resort', and is called the self.[14] In the *KU* the *akṣara*$_1$ is compared with the root of the *peepal* tree like the tree analogy of the *BG* (XI.1). "The *akṣara*$_1$ is indestructible (*amṛtam*)."[15] It is the Supreme *Puruṣa* being devoid of worldly attributes. One who knows this becomes free and attains immortality. The *Upaniṣads* describe this state as "not this, not this" (*BU* II.iii.6, III.ix.26), 'not gross, not subtle, not short' (*BU* III.viii.8). "It is the changeless, bodiless, inexpressible, unsupporting."[16] The *akṣara*$_1$ can't be denoted by substance and quality. Words can't describe it. Hence, it is indescribable.

> Where one sees nothing, hears nothing else, understands nothing else, that is the infinite... Verily, the infinite is the same as the immortal....[17]

The *BU* declares that "He is great, unborn etc," (IV.iv.25). This implies that all modifications are denied and this Brahman is absolutely immutable (*akṣara*$_1$). The *MU* clearly mentions the concept of *akṣara*$_1$ which is higher than the other *akṣara*$_2$ (called the unmanifested *Māyā*). The *akṣara*$_1$ is described negatively being devoid of all limiting adjuncts and it is like

11 Swami Gambhirananda. *Eight Upaniṣads*, Vol. II, p. 91. Delhi Entally Road, Calcutta-14, 1972. p. 201.

12 *Ibid.*, p. 115.

13 *Ibid.*, p. 169.

14 *Ibid.*, pp. 153-54.

15 *Ibid.*, 201.

16 *Ibid.*, p. 342.

17 S. Radhakrishnan, *The Principal Upaniṣads*, p. 486.

space, free from all forms. "It is supremely tranquil, eternal effulgence, divine absorption, immutable, and fearless."[18]

In order to describe the nature of the *akṣara*$_1$, Yājñavalkya in his reply to Gārgī says :

> Whosoever, O Gārgī, without knowing this Imperishable (*akṣara*) departs from the world, is pitiable.[19]

The *KU* takes it as the ancient (*purāṇaḥ*), undecaying (*śāśvataḥ*), eternal (*nityaḥ*) and birthless (*ajaḥ*). The intelligent Self is neither born nor does It die. It did not originate from anything, nor did anything originate from It.[20] It is beginningless (*anādi*), and infinite (*anantam*). It is soundless, touchless, undiminishing, tasteless, eternal, distinct from *Mahat* and ever constant.[21] That Immutable *Puruṣa* is the ātman, the self which leads us to immortality.[22] In the *MU*, we find that *akṣara*, is sometimes described as *akṣara-ātman* and sometimes as the *akṣara-puruṣa* (Immutable Self). This *akṣara-puruṣa* of the *MU* is identical with the *akṣara* concept of the *Gītā* (XII. 2-5). Unlike the *Praśna* and *Muṇḍaka*, the *ŚU* (I.i.9) takes the infinite Ātman as the *akṣara*$_1$ which includes in it both the *kṣara* and *akṣara* (*amṛtākṣara*). This *amṛtākṣara* of the *ŚU* is identical with the description of the *amṛtaḥ puruṣaḥ* (immortal *puruṣa*) that we notice in the *MU*.[23]

The *BU* describes the *amṛta puruṣa* as "the shinning, immortal person who is in this earth...is just this self. This is immortal, this is Brahman, this is All."[24] The *akṣara*$_1$ is ever attained. It is the summum bonum of the human life. It reveals its own nature. One attains this Supreme Self not by the *Vedas*, the scriptures, nor through intelligence,[25] nor through delusion,

18 Swami Gambhirananda, *Etghi Upaniṣads*, Vol.II, Advaita Ashrama, Calcutta 1972, p. 313.

19 S. Radhakrishnan, *The Principal Upaniṣads*, George Allen and Unwin Ltd., London, 1953, p. 233.

20 Swami Gambhirananda, *Eight Upaniṣads*, Vol. I, Advaita Ashrama, Calcutta 1972, p. 143.

21 *Ibid.*, p. 167.

22 Swami Gambhirananda, *Eight Upaniṣads*, Vol. II, p. 133.

23 *Ibid.*, pp. 106-7.

24 S. Radhakrishnan, *The Principal Upaniṣads*, p. 201.

25 Swami Gambhirananda, *Eight Upaniṣads*, Vol. II, 161.

nor through knowledge unassociated with monesticism[26] but by the discriminative knowledge (*Vivekajñāna*).

The *CU* further writes :

> The person who is seen in the eye, he is the Self. This is the immortal, the fearless, this is Brahman.[27]

There is no difference between the Ātman and Brahman. They qualify each other. Śaṅkara writes, commenting on the *MāU* :

> All this is, indeed, Brahman. This Ātman is Brahman.[28]

Hence, there is no difficulty in taking *akṣara*$_1$ as the Ātman, for the term Ātman, excludes the Brahman in the form of sun and other manifestations. In other words, *akṣara*$_1$ can be synonym of Ātman or the Supreme Brahman, not encased in the body by the limiting adjuncts.

Furthermore, in certain *Upaniṣads* we find the description of the term *Puruṣa* which appears to be similar with the *akṣara*$_1$. Whether the term *akṣara* and *puruṣa* are identical or they are two distinct categories is a controversial issue. Some scholars have tried to prove that they aim at the same goal, both being eternal and unborn. Others have attempted to identify the two. There is still a third opinion that the *Puruṣa* being personal is higher than the Impersonal *akṣara*.

In *BU*, we find that both these terms viz., the *Puruṣa* and the *akṣara* are being referred to independent of each other. Both the *MU* and the *ŚU* take *akṣara* and *puruṣa* as eternal and unborn.[29] They are the two different goals (*gati*), *akṣara* (*MU* II.2.3), *Puruṣa* (*MU* II.2.8), independent of each other (*ŚU* IV.18, I.II). The *MU* goes a step ahead in pointing out that the *puruṣa* is higher than the *akṣara* (*akṣarāt parataḥ paraḥ*)[30] and (*parāt paraḥ puruṣaḥ*).[31] Of course, there are passages in the *MU* which distinctly state that *puruṣa* is higher than *akṣara* (II.i.2,

26 Swami Gambhirananda, *Eight Upaniṣads*, p. 162.

27 S. Radhakrishnan, *The Principal Upaniṣads*, p. 416.

28 Swami Nikhilananda, *The Upaniṣads*, Phoneix House Ltd., London, 1957, p. 224.

29 Swami Gambhirananda, *Eight Upaniṣads*, Vol. II, p. 89.

30 *Ibid*, p. 115.

31 *Ibid.*, pp. 168-69.

III.2.8). These two passages of the *MU* clearly show that *puruṣa* being essentially transcendental and formless (*nāmarūpāt vimuktaḥ*) is superior to the (other) superior immutable (*Māyā*) i.e. the *akṣara*.

Śaṅkara writes here that the other superior immutable is none else but the *akṣara which* is conditioned by the adjuncts. This conditioned *akṣara* is not *Nirgṇa* Brahman of Śaṅkara. It stands for the concept $akṣara_2$ of the *Upaniṣads* and this $akṣara_2$ is higher than all modifications (*vikāras*), *akṣarāt parataḥ* being the seed of all the effects and occasions and at the same time lower than the $akṣara_1$ or the Supreme *Puruṣa*. *Puruṣa* (*divya puruṣa*) which is self-effulgent is described as *param* (higher), *parāt* than the higher ($akṣara_2$). To support this argument, one can take a note of the *PU* and *ŚU* which aim at the same direction.

In *PU*[32] there is the description of two Brahmans, the superior and the inferior in relation to Om (*param ca aparam ca*), the superior one is Immutable, devoid of all adjuncts and is called *Puruṣa* and the inferior is called *Prāṇa* (V.2). This 'Superior Brahman is higher than the higher one (viz., the *Hiraṇyagarbha*, writes Śaṅkara.[33] Śaṅkara marks here no distinction between the *akṣara* and *Puruṣa*.

> That by Immutable is referred to by the word *Puruṣa* because of all pervasiveness or existence in all the hearts and that again is *satyam*, true, because of being essentially the Supreme Reality, and it is *akṣara* (Immutable, because of the absence of mutation, injury and decay).[34]

Even though Śaṅkara has not pointed out here whether this *akṣara* refers to the *Nirguṇa* Brahman or to *Īśvara* yet from the nature of the description, it is understood that in this passage, *akṣara* refers to $akṣara_1$. In another passage of the same *Upaniṣad*, it is said "Then there is the higher (knowledge)

32 Swami Gambhirananda, *Eight Upaniṣads*, Vol. II, Advaita Ashrama Calcutta, 1972, p. 470

33 *Ibid.*, p. 474.

34 *Ibid.*, p. 112.

by which is realised that Immutable,"[35] which implies that between the *akṣara* and the *Puruṣa*, there is not much of difference. Śaṅkara would mean by the (higher) knowledge the knowledge of the Brahman, (*tat akṣaram adhigamyate*), which helps one to attain the *akṣara* (Immutable). In *KU*, we come across the description of such a *Puruṣa* which is Brahman (*akṣara*$_1$).

> *Puruṣa*, who keeps awake and goes on creating desirable things even when the senses fall asleep, is pure; and He is Brahman, and He is called the Immortal. All the worlds are fixed on Him; none can transcend Him. This is that.[36]

In the *ŚU* (I.B), we find the description of such *akṣara*$_1$ who is Supreme, who supports both the mutable (*kṣara*) and the immutable (*akṣara*), the manifest (*vyakta*) and the unmanifest (*avyakta*).

(*B*) *Māyā-Śakti* (*Akṣara*$_2$)

Akṣara has been used in different senses in the *Upaniṣads*. I have discussed *akṣara*$_1$ in my previous section which has been taken as the *Nirguṇa* Brahman. At present, I would like to discuss various Upaniṣadic passages, wherein *akṣara*$_2$ is used.

Śaṅkara interprets this term as the *māyā-śakti* or the *Kūṭasthā-Puruṣa*. The term *māya-śakti* is used as the *devātma-śakti* in *ŚU*.[37] The power (*śakti*) is not different from the *Śaktimān* (the Lord) but is hidden in it.[38] The *devātmaśakti* is of the nature of the Supreme. The power of manifestation (*māyā-śakti*) is in the form of *Īśvara* which is hidden by the qualities of *sattva*, *rajas* and *tamas* writes Radhakrishnan.[39]

Śaṅkara interprets these three as fire (*tapas*), water (*apaḥ*)

35 Swami Gambhirananda, *Eight Upaniṣads*, Vol. II, Advaita Ashrama, Calcutta, 1972, p. 97.

36 *Ibid.*, p. 191.

37 S. Radhakrishnan, *The Principal Upaniṣads*, George Allen and Unwin Ltd., London, 1953. p. 710.

38 *Ibid.*, p. 710.

39 *Ibid.*, p. 710.

and food (*annam*).[40] Śaṅkara's interpretation actually refers to the subtle elements of the *CU* (VI.2.3-4, VI.3), which are brought forth by the pure Being (*Sat*) for the creation of the universe.[41]

> The powers by which *Īśvara* creates the world of diversity is known...variously in the *Upaniṣad*. It is known as *Māyā*, *Īśānī*, *Aja*, *Pradhāna*, *Jāla*, *Śakti*, *Avidyā*, *Bhogyam*, and *Prakṛti*.[42]

But this so-called power of the Lord (*māyā*) is not an independent entity in the *ŚU* like the Sāṅkhya's *Prakṛti*. It is an inseparable power of the Lord. *Īśvara* creates this world through the superimposition of *Māyā* on Him.[43] The 8th *śloka* of the 1st chapter of the same *Upaniṣad* points out that the term *avyakta akṣara* is the unmanifested *māyā-śakti*. On the other hand, Śaṅkara writes :

> The manifested world is due to the power of *māyā* which is not independent of Brahman and so does not constitute a second to it.[44]

While commenting on the 9th *śloka* of the 4th *Adhyāya* of this *Upaniṣad*, Śaṅkara makes it clear that the *kūṭastha-akṣara* creates the unmanifested world by his *śakti* (power)...... *māyī sṛjate*.[45] Here the *kūṭastha prakṛti* is designated as *māyā* and *Īśvara* is the *māyin*.[46] The 1st *śloka* of the 5th chapter of the same *Upaniṣad* states :

> In the imperishable, infinite highest Brahman are the two, knowledge and ignorance, placed hidden. Ignorance is perishable while knowledge is immortal. And he who controls knowledge and ignorance is another (distinct from either).[47]

40 Balbir Singh, *The Conceptual Framework of Indian Philosophy*, The Macmillan Company of India Ltd., Delhi, 1976, p. 195.

41 *Ibid.*, p. 195.

42 *Ibid.*, p. 195.

43 S. Radhakrishnan, *The Principal Upaniṣads*, p. 734.

44 *Ibid.*, p. 715.

45 *Śaṅkarabhāṣya*, Gītā Press, Gorakhpur, p. 116.

46 *Ibid.*, p. 117.

47 S. Radhakrishnan., *The Principal Upaniṣads*, George Allen and Unwin Ltd., London, 1953. p. 738.

Here, the term *dve akṣare* stands for *vidyā* (knowledge) and *avidyā* (ignorance). *Vidyā* refers to *amṛta* or *akṣara* and *avidyā* to *kṣara*. These two are hidden in unmanifested form in another i.e. $akṣara_1$, which is distinct from either.

Radhakrishnan interprets *vidyā* which stands for the knowledge of 'one' and the *avidyā* for the knowledge of 'many'.[48] This knowledge of the 'one' is the unmanifested *Prakṛti* which is the cause of the world. In verse 8 of the same *Upaniṣad*, *kṣara* is designated as *vyakta* (manifest) in contrast with the term *akṣara* as *avyakta* (unmanifest). Beyond these both *vyakta* and *avyakta* there is the Supreme Lord which refers to $akṣara_1$. And the term *avyakta-akṣara* stands for $akṣara_2$ or the *Māyā-śakti*.[49]

The *ŚU* further explains that the *māyā* as the power of the *Īśvara*.[50] It is the *māyā* and *puruṣa* is the *māyīn*, one who possesses *māyā*[51] (IV.10). Here, the term *māyā* refers to $akṣara_2$ and *puruṣa* is something different from the $akṣara_2$. This *māyā-śakti* or the *devātma-śakti* is the cause of the world and this *māyā-śakti* is the other aspect of *Īśvara*. (*Īśvara-rūpeṇa avasthitam*). *Īśvara* by this power creates, preserves and dissolves the world (I.3).[52] Thus, Brahman conceived as *Īśvara*, endowed with *māyā*, is held responsible for this phenomenal world. It is through *māyā* that *akṣara* seems to be the material as well as the efficient cause of the world. This *akṣara* appears to be *Jīvātman* because of *māyā-śakti*. Thus, the *akṣara* is the abode of both *Īśvara* and *Jīva*.

> With regard to *Īśvara*, the whole universe is the limiting adjunct, whereas with the *Jīva*, the individual body is the limiting adjunct. It is Brahman alone who, in association with collective *māyā*, appears as the universe and in association with individual *māyā*, appears as the *Jīva*.[53]

48 S. Radhakrishnan, *The Principal Upaniṣads*, George Allen and Unwin Ltd., London, 1953 p. 738.

49 *Ibid.*, p. 714.

50 *Ibid.*, p. 725.

51 *Ibid.*, p. 734.

52 *Ibid.*, p. 710.

53 Swami Nikhilānanda., *The Upaniṣads*, Phoneix House Ltd.,London, 1957, p. 80.

The *ŚU* discusses the nature of this *Jīvātman* as 'bound' because of his being an enjoyer.[54] Enjoyment is being superimposed on the *Jīvātman* because of *māyā*......like the rope-snake illustration.

In the *MU* we find the mention of these two distinct categories of *akṣara* out of which one is the higher immutable (i.e., *akṣara*$_1$) and the other is called the unmanifested (*Māyā*) which is itself higher than its own modifications being devoid of all limiting adjuncts.

> *Puruṣa* is transcendental, since He is formless. And since He is co-extensive with all that is external and internal and since He is birthless, therefore He is without vital force and without mind; He is pure and superior to the (other) superior immutable (*Māyā*).[55]

Here, *akṣara*$_1$ is higher than the (other) higher immutable (*akṣara*$_2$) called the unmanifested (*Māyā*). This *māyā* is the limiting adjunct of Brahman which causes the appearance of causality in Brahman. It appears to be the seed of all the effects and accessories, writes Śaṅkara.[56]

> As rivers, flowing down, become indistinguishable on reaching the sea by giving up their names and forms, so also the illumined soul, having become freed from name and form, reaches the self-effulgent *Puruṣa* that is higher than the higher (*Māyā*).[57]

Here, the term *divyam puruṣam* (self-effulgent self i.e., *akṣara*$_1$) is higher than the higher (*Māyā*) i.e., *akṣara*$_2$.

> As a spider sends forth and draws in ((its thread), as herbs grow on the earth, as the hair (grows) on the head and the body of a living person, so from the Imperishable arises here the universe.[58]

54 S. Radhakrishnan., *The Principal Upaniṣads*, p. 714.

55 Swami Gambhirananda, *Eight Upanisads*, Vol. II., Advaita Ashrama, Calcutta, 1972, p. 115.

56 *Ibid.*, pp. 116-17.

57 *Ibid.*, pp. 168-69.

58 S. Radhakrishnan., *The Principal Upaniṣads*, George Allen and Unwin Ltd., London, 1953, p. 673.

Here, the Imperishable (*akṣara*) is taken as the sole cause of this universe. *Kāraṇāntaraṁ anapekṣya svayam eva sṛjate*, writes Śaṅkara. In the same *Upaniṣad* it is again said :

> The self-effulgent Self imagines Itself through Itself by the power of Its own *Māyā*. The Self Itself cognises the objects.[59]

Here, the term *devaḥ ātmā* (the self-effulgent self) which through Its own *Māyā* manifests the unmanifested objects like earth etc., which stands for *akṣara*$_2$. The Lord Himself seems to be deluded by His own *Māyā* as the magical spell, created by the magicians, makes the very clear sky appear as though filled with leafy trees in bloom, writes Śaṅkara[60] (*ātmā māyā-visarjitaḥ*). But this *māyā* does not exist in reality. The *akṣara*$_2$ differentiates through *māyā* like the moon seen as many by a jaundiced eye, says Śaṅkara.[61] It becomes manifest only through *Māyā*.

> There is no diversity here, and the Lord on account of *Māyā* (is perceived) as manifold...He is born on account of *Māyā* alone.[62]

"The Lord on account of *Māyā* (is perceived as manifold)" says the *BU* (II.5.19). It is said "He goes from death to death who sees multiplicity as it were, in It" (*KU* II.i.11). Thus "It can reasonably have birth in the form of the universe through *Māyā* like the illusion of a snake on a rope; but this birthless Self can't have birth in the real sense", writes Śaṅkara.[63]

> The entities that are born thus are not born in reality. Their birth is as that of a thing through *Māyā* (magic). And that *Māyā* again has no reality.[64]

The unmanifested *Prakṛti* has been discussed in the *KU* as such "The unmanifested is higher than *Mahat*; *Puruṣa* is

59 Swami Gambhirananda, *Eight Upaniṣads*, Vol. II, Advaita Ashrama Calcutta, 1972. p. 242.
60 *Ibid.*, p. 248.
61 *Ibid.*, p. 293.
62 *Ibid.*, p. 297.
63 *Ibid*, p. 304.
64 *Ibid.*, p. 371.

higher than the unmanifested. There is nothing nigher than *Puruṣa*...''[65]. Here the unmanifested which is the cause of the whole manifested world of names and forms is called *avyakta* (unmanifested)...*avyākṛta* (unevolved)...*ākāśa* (space), etc., and this *avyakta* is taken here as *akṣara*$_2$. The *TU* states that the formed and the formless, existing in the Self in their state of unmanifested name and form, are manifested by the indwelling Self.''[66] Beyond this *avyakta* (i.e., *akṣara*$_2$) is *Puruṣa. Puruṣa* is superior to the unmanifested.[67] It is the Supreme goal (*parā gatiḥ*), is higher than the *avyakta*. By *avyakta* Śaṅkara understands not the *Prakṛti* of Śāṅkhya but the *Māyā-śakti* which is responsible for the whole world including personal God.[68]

The *akṣara*$_2$ (*Māyā-śakti*) is hidden in all beings and is covered by *avidyā* i.e. *Māyā*, which is unreal and it is through *Māyā* of the Lord everybody moves through birth and death.[69] The *TU* says :

> In the beginning all this was but the unmanifested (Brahman). From that emerged the manifested... .[70]

If the imperishable actually becomes the multiferious forms of the world, then it should cease to remain imperishable and immutable. But this is certainly not plausible as the imperishable can never go perishable and perishable can never become imperishable.[71] Ātman, through his inseparable power of *Māyā* manifested the whole universe of multiplicity of two categories: the animate and the inanimate (*BU* II.5. 19). Hence, the birth of the imperishable Ātman or His becoming the multiplicity is possible only through *Māyā*, it can't be transformed.[72]

Thus, the *akṣara*$_2$ is the supreme resort and is called the self. It is hidden in all creatures from *Brahman* to a clump of grass Only one who acquires 'discriminating knowledge under-

65 Swami Gambhirananda, *Eight Upaniṣads*, Vol. I, Advaita Ashrama, Calcutta, 1972, p. 160.

66 *Ibid.*, p. 339.

67 *Ibid.*, p. 206.

68 S. Radhakrishnan, *The Principal Upaniṣads*, p. 626.

69 Swami Gambhirananda, *Eight Upaniṣads* Vol. I, p. 163.

70 *Ibid.*, p. 341.

71 Swami Gambhirananda., *Eight Upaniṣads*, Vol. II, p. 294,

72 *Ibid.*, p. 371

stands the nature of this *pratyagātman*, the indwelling self. The *pratyagātman* is not affected by the sorrows of the world : "*na lipyate lokaduḥkhena*". It seems so only because of ignorance just as 'snake-rope', 'silver-mother of pearl', 'water and desert', etc., writes Śaṅkara. This *pratyagātman* devoid of *māyā-śakti* is transcendental and immutable (*akṣara*)$_1$.

(*C*) *Praṇava* (*Akṣara*$_3$)

In the history of Indian Philosophical literature, the word *Om* or *praṇava* is very significant. It is sometimes designated as the *akṣara*...the immutable, imperishable and the undecayable one and sometimes as the letter of the alphabet. *Om* is the symbol of the Supreme Spirit. The one letter, *Om* is the emblem of the Supreme Being, says the *Gītā*. When we analyse this word, we find that it is a triliteral word consisting of '*a*', '*u*', '*m*'. It is known as symbol of assent in ordinary parlance as well as in the Vedic literature. One who meditates on this syllable attains all the desirable ends. By meditating on this *Oṁkāra*, which is the emblem of the truthful Supreme Brahman...the all pervasive one, one attains immortality. That's why it is said in the *Upaniṣad* that "verily, the syllable *Om* is all this...yea, the syllable *Om* is verily all this."[73] (*CU*, III. 23.3) Śaṅkara understands Brahman as the *Praṇava* or *Om*. But this word *Praṇava* is used in the *Upaniṣads* very ambiguously.

In the *CU* the word *Udgītha* is used as a substitute for *Om*. Almost all the Vedic chants start with this word *Om*. "He who meditates upon this syllable of assent as *Udgītha* (endowed with the quality of prosperity) verily becomes one who increases all the desirable ends."[74] The word *Om* represents the inferior Brahman (*Hiraṇyagarbha*). *etat eva akṣaram Barhma*, as well as the Supreme Brahaman *etat eva akṣaraṁ param*.

73 Swami Swahananda, *The CU*, Ramkrishna Math Publication, Madras, 1956, p. 159.

74 *Ibid.*, 1956, p. 12.

The *KU* describes these two aspects of *akṣara* in the light of attaining the inferior Brahman and knowing the Supreme Brahman.[75] This implie that the inferior Brahman constitutes a fraction of *Praṇava* which can be attained by means of meditation and worship. The aspirants of this type can at best attain the *akṣara*$_4$ and they are the devotees of the medium and dull intellect. It is repeatedly said in the *upaniṣads* that *Om* is Brahman. *Om* is all this. *Om iti idam sarvam* (*TU* I.viii.i).

The *MU* compares *praṇava*, the syllable *Om*, with a bow[76] by which the individual souls enter into the Immutable. The conditioned self, when purified by the syllable *Om* repeatedly merges in Brahman and is devoid of all obstacles. "That goal which all the *Vedas* with one voice propound, which all the austerities speak of, and wishing of which people practise *Brahmacarya*...it is this viz., *Om*".[77] Thus *Praṇava* is instrument for attaining the inferior as well as the Supreme Brahman.[78]

The *MāU* takes *Om* as all this. *Om iti etat akṣaraṁ idaṁ sarvam.* "All that is past, present, or future is verily *Om*. And whatever is beyond the three periods of time is also verily *Om*"[79] (*sarvaṁ oṁkārah eva*). Śaṅkara illucidates this point by stating that all the nameable objects as well as the names are identical in nature. And the Supreme Brahman is known by means of this identity. So it is *praṇava*, *Om*. This Brahman again is beyond this identity as It differs from both the name and the nameable objects. One attains this Brahman by constant meditation. But that one which is beyond this 'identity' represents 'the Supreme Brahman (*akṣara*$_1$).

In the *MāU* the word *Om* has been discussed in detail by splitting up it into three different letters viz.,...'*a*', '*u*', '*m*' Vaiśvānara (*Virāṭ*) having the waking state as His sphere of

75 Swami Gambhirananda., *Eight Upaniṣads*, Vol. I, Advaita Aśhrama, Calcutta, 1972. p. 142.

76 Swami Gambhirananda., *Eight Upaniṣads*, Val. II, Advaita Aśhrama, Calcutta, 1972. p. 132.

77 Swami Gambhirananda., *Eight Upaniṣads*, Vol. I, p. 140.

78 *Ibid.*, p 142.

79 Swami Gambhirananda., *Eight Upaniṣads*, Vol. II, p. 179.

activity is called *akāraḥ*, *a*...the first letter of *Om*...which pervades all speech.[80] The Vedic text spports this view. "The sound *a* is indeed all speech" (*AiĀ* II iii.7). *Taijasa* *Hirṇya-garbha*) having the dream state as His sphere of activty is the second letter *ukāraḥ*, *u* of *Om*, because of the similarity of excellence and intermediateness. This letter is intermediate in between *a* and *m* and hence it is related to both.[81] *Prājña* having the deep sleep state as His sphere of activity is the last letter *makāraḥ*, *m* of *Om*.. because of pronouncement and absorption finally.[82] From the above analysis it follows that the 'etter *a* stands for the gross universe, the waking state (*Viśva*), '*u*' stands for the subtle universe (*Taijasa*), the dream state, and *m* represents the deep sleep state (causal state), *Prājña*. Everything is reduced to *Om* and all the three states of meditations relate to *Om*. The partless *Om* in *Turīya*...beyond all conventional dealings, the limit of negation of the phenomenal world, the auspicious, and the non-dual."[83] This *Turīya* state represents the absolute self which is completely devoid of all empirical dealings and it is the *akṣara*$_1$. The rest three represent the inferior Brahman i.e. the *akṣara*$_4$. Thus in my view *Praṇavaḥ* in the *Upaniṣads* stands for either *akṣara*$_1$ or *akṣara*$_4$. The aspirants of the average intellect make the distinctions of the three letters and quarters called as "the three stages of life".[84] But a man having above knowledge maditates on this *Praṇava* fearlessly as it is the Supreme Reality (*Brahma nirbhayam*). "The enlightened man is not afraid of anything" (*TU* II.ix.l). And this Supreme Reality is attained when the letters and the quarters disappear. The *GPK* describes it "as without cause, without inside and outside, and without effect; and it is undecaying."[85] *Om* is known as God (*Īśvara*) existing in the hearts of all beings. It is *Śivaḥ* (auspicious), because of

80 Swami Gambhirananda, *Eight Upaniṣads*, Advaita Ashrama Calcutta, Vol. II, p. 220.

81 *Ibid.*, p. 221.

82 *Ibid.*, p. 222.

83 *Ibid.*, p. 226.

84 *Ibid.*, p. 289.

85 *Ibid.*, p. 229.

negations of all duality, having infinite dimentions (*anantamātraḥ*).[86]

The *PU* emphasises on the intense meditation (*abhidhyāna*) on *Om* by withdrawing the internal organs from external objects and observing moral injunctions till death. One attains "this very Brahman, that is (known as) the inferior and superior,"[87] through the same means alone, i.e., *Om* (*paraṁ ca aparaṁ ca*). The superior one is Immutable and is called *Puruṣa* or *akṣara*$_1$, and the inferior one, the First Born, called *Prāṇa*, is but *Om*. But in fact, this superior and inferior Brahman can't be known directly, being devoid of all distinctions created by attributes. Hence, Brahman which is both inferior and superior is *Om* in a secondary sense, says Śaṅkara. One who meditates on *Om* attains either of the two for *Om* is the symbol of Brahman. Śaṅkara interprets the 5th *śloka* of the 5th chapter of the the same *Upaniṣad* as "anyone who meditates on the Supreme *Puruṣa* with the help of this very syllable *Om*, as possessed of three letters, becomes unified in the Sun, consisting of light."[88] Here the Supreme *Puruṣa* refers to the *Saguṇa* Brahman which is described in the *Vedas* as dwelling in the solar orb[89] (*Om iti tena eva akṣareṇa*). This passage of the *PU* clearly states that the Supreme *Puruṣa* is higher than the *Praṇava*, *Om*...the *Hiraṇyagarbha*. Śaṅkara's mistake probably would be here in taking *praṇava* as simply *akṣara* without mentioning the category of *akṣara* to which it belongs. The Supreme *Puruṣa*, being *Param parāt*, is superior to the higher one. It is included in the category of *akṣara*$_1$. The *Praṇava* helps an intelligent man to attain the threefold world, which represents the inferior Brahman and again with the help of *Om* one attains the Supreme Brahman which is immutable, free and is called *Puruṣa*, the all-pervasive, which is *sanātana*, quiet, free, devoid of all such distinctions as waking, dream, and sleep and is transcendental to the whole universe, and is

86 Swami Gambhirananda, *Eight Upaniṣads*, Advita Ashrama, Vol. II, p. 231.

87 *Ibid.*, p. 470.

88 *Ibid.*, p 474.

89 *Ibid*, p. 474.

therefore *ajaram*, free from old age, *amṛtam*. beyond death, and consequently *abhayam* fearless.[90]

The *ŚU* takes *praṇava* as the lower self.. the *akṣara*$_4$ "*praṇavo hy aparaṁ brahma.*" The self (lower) though unperceived is perceived by constant meditation on the syllable *Om*, just like the fire in the fire-wood is not visible at first, though it is there in its subtle form.[91] The self, the Supreme Self can't be known through the *Praṇava* for it is devoid of all attributes and characteristics. It is not to be worshipped as the symbol for Brahman can't be brought down to the level of the symbol. It should be meditated through the symbol. The symbol is to be transformed into Supreme Self.[92] Thus, meditating on the Supreme Self through *praṇava*, one realises the *akṣara*$_1$ and meditating the lower self through *Praṇava*[93] one attains the *akṣara*$_4$. *Om* thus, stands for both the *Nirguṇa* Brahman and the *Īśvara*. Gauḍapāda writes that *Praṇava* is the *apara*-Brahman (lower Brahman) and if we worship *Om* as *Īśvara* we overcome sorrows "*praṇavaṁ hīśvaraṁ vidyat*". It is also the *para* Brahman (higher Brahman).[94] The *Maitrī Upaniṣad* says, "This syllable '*Om*', verily, is the higher and the lower Brahman"[95] (VI. 5). It is said "This syllable, indeed is holy, the syllable, indeed is Supreme. By knowing that syllable, indeed, whatever one desires (becomes) his.[96] (VI. 4)

2. *THE BRAHMA-SŪTRA*

Like the *Upaniṣads* and the *Gītā*, the *Sūtrakāra* also uses this concept ambiguously in the *Brahma-Sūtra*. Even Śaṅkara's interpretation sometimes seems to be very much confusing.

90 Swami Gambhirananda, *Eight Upaniṣads*, Vol. II. p. 478-479.

91 S. Radhakrishnan, *The Principal Upaniṣads*, George Allen and Unwin Ltd., London, 1953. p. 717.

92 Swami Nikhilananda, *The Upaniṣads*, Phoneix House Ltd., London, 1957. p. 188.

93 S. Radhakrishnan, *The Principal Upaniṣads*, p. 703.

94 *Ibid.*, p. 703.

95 *Ibid.*, p. 819.

96 *Ibid.*, p. 818.

Akṣara is designated as *Nirguṇa* Brahman in the *Brahma-Sūtra*. The *Nirguṇa* aspect of *akṣara* refers to *akṣara*$_1$. The *Bhūman* of the *Upaniṣads* is taken as *akṣara* (the Supreme Self).[97] "That is *Bhūman* where one does not see anything else does not know anything else" (*CU* VII. xxiv. 1). This *Bhūman* is *amṛta*. It exists by its own glory. Śaṅkara interprets that both in the *CU* and in the *BU* (III.8.7) *Bhūman* is taken as *akṣara*$_1$ (the Supreme Self). "It is neither gross, nor subtle, neither small nor big, etc." (*BU* III.8.8). "On this *Akṣara*, O Gārgī, is the (unmanifest) space woven and transfixed" (*BU* III.8.11). This *akṣara* is the Supreme Brahman, imperishable, all-pervasive, eternal and omnipresence "*Akṣaraṁ ambarāntadhṛteḥ*".[98] Here, *akṣara* refers to the Supreme Self "because of supporting all things up to (and including) space." The act of supporting belongs to *Parameśvara* because of his mighty rule.[99] "Under the mighty rule of this *Akṣara* (Immutable), O Gārgī, the sun and the moon, are held in their positions etc." (*BU* III.viii.9).

The *Sūtrakāra* subsequently mentions that *Akṣara* means Brahman because of the act of holding all things including space. The *śruti* says :

> The *Akṣara* is never seen, but is the witness. It is never heard, but is the hearer ; It is never thought of, but is the thinker ; It is never known, but is the knower[100] (*BU* III.8.11).

Śaṅkara writes, here *akṣara* stands neither for the embodied soul nor for the insentient *Pradhāna*. It means Brahman. In the *śruti* (*PU* V.2.7) we find that *akṣara* refers to both *parā* and *aparā* Brohman. But *sūtrakāra* categoricdlly says that *akṣara* stands for *Parā*-Brahman, 'because of the object of seeing' (*īkṣaṇa*)[101]. *Akṣara* is the object of seeing' and of 'meditation'. It is 'higher than the higher'. The *KU* says, "There is nothing higher than *Puruṣa* (the all-pervading entity). He is the

97 Swami Gambhirananda., *Brahma-Sūtra-Bhāṣya*, Advaita Ashram, Calcutta 1972. p. 167.

98 *Ibid.*, p. 175.

99 *Ibid.*, p. 176.

100 S. Radhakrishnan, *The Principal Upaniṣads*, p. 233.

101 Swami Gambhirananda., *Brahma-Sūtra-Bhāṣya*, p. 177.

culmination. He is the highest goal" (I.3.11). Śaṅkara interprets the Supreme *Puruṣa* is the Supreme Brahman which is to be meditated on with the help of *Om*. The Supreme Brahman can't have contradictory qualities. It is the attributeless Brahman which is unchangeable, is to be taken as *akṣara*$_1$ and not the opposite. The *Śruti* also supports this view. "Brahman is soundless, touchless, colourless, undiminishing" (*KU* I.iii.15). *Sūtrakāra* writes :

> Not even according to place can Brahman have a twofold characteristics, for everywhere (It is taught to be without attributes).[102] (*BSB* III.ii.11).

The *Sūtrakāra* further writes that Brahman is formless, as that is the dominant note of the *Upaniṣads*.[103] "It is neither gross, nor minute, neither short nor long" (*BU* III.viii.8), "*Puruṣa* is transcendental, since He is co-extensive with all that is external and internal, since He is birthless"(*MU* II.i.2). "That Brahman is without prior or posterior, without interior and exterior. The self, the perceiver of everything, is Brahman" *BU* II.v.9).

The Supreme Brahman who is essentially formless adores form entering into the limiting adjuncts such as bodies etc. We find references, to this type of Brahman both in the *Śrutis* and *Smṛtis*. The Brahman having the attributes is called, *apara* Brahman or *Īśvara* (i.e. *akṣara*$_4$). Thus, both in the *Śrutis* and in the *Smṛtis* we find the mention of Brahman having both form and formless. But this description of Brahman does not involve any contradiction, for Śaṅkara points out that the Brahman having form is a stopping stone to the formless Brahman (*akṣara*$_1$) through a sublation of the manifested universe.[104] This manifested form of the Brahman is meant for the meditation of the dull intellect. Thus, both these manifest and unmanifested forms are the two different aspects of the same reality. Brahman is unmanifest (*avyakta*), say the *Śruti* and the *Smṛti*. "It is not comprehended through the eye, nor

102 Swami Gambhirananda, *Brahma-Sūtra-Bhāṣya*, p. 609.
103 *Ibid.*, p. 632.
104 *Śaṅkarabhāṣya*, Gītā Press, Gorakhpur p. 262.

through speech, nor through the other senses, nor is it attained through austerity or *karma*" (*MU* III. i.3). "The Self is imperceptible, for it is never perceived" (*BU* III.ix.26). It is not this, not this (*BU* II.iii.6). "He is said to be undetermined, unthinkable, immutable" (*BGB* II.25). From the above passages, it is understood that Brahman is *avyakta* (i.e. $akṣara_2$) which is *amūrta*. The *BU* distinguishes *amūrta* from *mūrat*. *Amūrta* is *parāprakṛti* and *mūrta* is *aparā-prakṛti* of the Lord. The Supreme Lord ($akṣara_1$) which is the abode of the two......the *vyakta* and the *avyakta*, is superior to both.[105] When the Brahman is in the effect state (*Kāraṇāvāsthā*) it possesses both the *parā* and *aparā prakṛti* in the unmanifest form, and it is the *nirguṇa* aspect of the Lord as discussed in the *śruti*. This has been confirmed by the aphorism "*pratiśedḥācca*".

> And on account of the denial[106] (*BSB* III.ii.30). Similarly from the denial of everything also (it follows that there is nothing but Brahman)[107] (*BSB* III.ii.36).

Besides this, we very often come across the description of *Saguṇa* Brahman (*Īśvara*) which is the cause of this manifested universe. *Īśvara* or the *Puruṣottama* thus stands for $akṣara_4$. This Brahman is to be meditated for it remains within the cavity of the heart (*IU* I.ii.2, *TU* II.1). It is the highest goal. It is the internal Ruler. It is the source of all creation. The *Sūtrakāra* further writes that *Akṣara* is Brahman. It supports all things, from earth to space.[108] "This act of supporting is possible for God only owing to the mention of His mighty rule" (*BSB* I.iii. 11). Here *akṣara* stands for *Īśvara*. This aspect of *akṣara* (i.e., $akṣara_4$) has been discussed vividly in the whole of *Brahma-Sūtra* as the *kārya Brahman* (*apara* Brahman) which is endowed with *māyā-śakti* to create this manifested universe. When the Brahman is in the causal state......its two natures : *parā* and *aparā* are manifested in different name and form. These two natures are two powers of the Supreme Self (*Īśvara*). Thus, the

105 *Śaṅkarabhāṣya*, Gītā Press, Gorakhpur, p. 263.

106 Swami Gambhirananda, *Brahma-Sūtra-Bhāṣya*, Advaita Ashrama Calcutta, 1972, p. 632.

107 *Ibid.*, p. 638,

108 *Ibid.*, p. 174.

Supreme Self is both *saguṇa* and *nirguṇa*. It is both *vyakta* and *avyakta*.[109]

On the basis of this some scholars have tried to point out that there are two distinct ultimate realities......the *akṣara* and the *puruṣa* and accordingly there are two types of worship (*upāsanā*)...the *akṣara* and the *puruṣa upāsanā*. But this is not the right interpretation. Śaṅkara interprets that these are the two different modes of worship of the same Lord.[110]

Avyakta is taken in the *Brahma-Sūtra* as a synonym of *akṣara* (i.e., *akṣara*$_2$), but not of *Pradhāna* of the Śāṅkhyas.[111] It is discussed in the *KU* that "The sense organs are higher than the senses, and mind is higher than the sense-objects but the intellect is higher than mind and the Great soul is higher than the intellect" (I.3.10). "The Unmanifest is higher than *Mahat*, *Puruṣa* is higher than the Unmanifest. There is nothing higher than *Puruṣa* (I.3.11)." Here, the term *mahān-ātmā* stands for the inner Self (*Jīvātman*). Beyond this *mahān-ātmā* is the *avyakta* (unmanifested) which is the cause of the world.[112] This *avyakta-akṣara* has been discussed from *BS* I.iv.1-7. "The subtle one...the body in its causal state...is sought to be spoken of...for the subtle cause is *avyakta*." "The universe was then undifferentiated", says the *Śruti* (*BU* I.iv.1) devoid of name and form. The *māyā-śakti* is not different from the Lord. The Lord can't work without His *śakti* (power of *Māyā*). This *māyā-śakti* is mentioned by the word unmanifest (*avyakta*), writes Śaṅkara. In the *Śruti*, the term *Avyakta* is used differently. It is sometimes referred to space, as stated in the text. "By the Immutable, O Gārgī is (the unmanifest) space pervaded" (*BU* III.8.11); sometimes it is called the immutable as in 'Higher than the higher immutable' (*MU* II.i.2); sometimes it is called *Māyā* as in, "Know *Māyā* to be Nature and the master of *Māyā* to be the great God" (*ŚU* IV.10). That *Māyā* is unmanifest for it can neither be real nor unreal.[113]

109 *Śaṅkarabhāṣya*, Gītā Press, Gorakhpur, p. 148.
110 *Ibid.*, p. 296.
111 *Ibid.*, p. 98.
112 *Ibid.*, p. 99.
113 Swami Gambhirananda., *Brahma-Sūtra-Bhāṣya*, p. 249

Nowhere in the text it is said that the *avyakta* is to be worshipped or to be known, says Śaṅkara. This word is used to reveal the nature of *Viṣṇu*.[114] The aphorism *samākarṣāt* (*BS* I.iv.15) rightly suggests that *akṣara* exists in the unmanifested form and 'non-existence' is used here in the secondary sense, interpretes Śaṅkara. Here, non-existance does not mean void because of its allusion (to Brahman).[115] In the *TU* (2.7) '*asadvā idamagra āsīt*' or in the *CU* (III.19.1) *Āditya Brahma*...the word *asat* is used not in the sense of void or unreal but it stands for the unmanifested Brahman (*akṣara*$_2$) and out of this, the manifest universe came into being. The *BU* uses the word *avyākṛta* (unevolved) in stead of *asat* (1.4.7) which means unmanifested (*aprakaṭa*).[116] The manifasted universe before its origin and after its destruction was in the unmanifested as the power of the Lord.

Lastly, *akṣara* is also nsed in the sense of *Praṇava* in the *Brahma-Sūtra*. This *akṣara* (i.e., *akṣara*$_3$) is to be worshipped as it is the Supreme Brahman. The *Śruti* says : "One who meditates on this three lettered *Om* becomes unified in the Sun. He is lifted up to the world of Brahman (*PU* V.5)". Śaṅkara finds no difference between the Supreme *Puruṣa* and the Supreme Brahman.[117] *Om* is synonymous with *Udgītha*, says the *Śruti*. "This *Udgītha* (its part '*Om*') is this space and it is great and higher than all that is high" (*CU* I.ix 2). It is the infinite, the Brahman (*akṣara*$_3$). *Om* is a means for the realization of the Brahman, writes Śaṅkara. The *Udgītha* meditation in the *CU* and the *BU* are not different at all.[118] There is a difference only in starting the meditation, interpretes Śaṅkara. The *CU* begins with "Let one meditate on the letter *Om* as *Udgītha* (I i.1). Here emphasis is laid on *Om*, a letter forming a part of *Udgītha*. But in the *BU* there is no question of part of the *Udgītha*. It is presented as a whole (along with all its parts), writes Śaṅkara. The *Sūtrakāra* writes : Since *Om*

114 Swami Gambhirananda, *Brahma-Sūtra-Bhāṣya*, p. 252.
115 *Ibid.*, p. 273.
116 *Śaṅkarabhāṣya*, Gītā Press, p. 110.
117 Swami Gambhirananda, *Brahma-Sūtra-Bhāṣya*, p. 180.
118 *Ibid.*, p. 652.

pervades all the *Vedas*, it is appropriate to qualify it by the word *Udgītha*.[119] "It is the essence of all essences, it is the highest, it is the symbol for the highest, and the eights in number" (*CU* I.i.3). In the 12th *śloka* of the 1st *pāda* of the 4th *Adhyāya* it is said that meditation on this *Praṇava* is to be repeated up till the moment of death for the scripture says so.[120] Satyakāma asks his teacher Pippalapāda 'one who meditates '*Om*' till death goes to which world ?' (*PU* 5.1). Pippalapāda says, 'one who meditates on two letters goes to the heaven (*Svargaloka*) (V. 3-4) and one who meditates the *dahara puruṣa* with the help of this *Om* goes to the *Puruṣa* residing in the Sun. Thus, Śaṅkara interpretes that one is suppose to worship this *Om* till death for the upliftment the people. But a devotee must meditate on it constantly, till death.[121] Otherwise, He may have rebirth, says the *Gītā* (VI.37-40).

3. *The Bhagavad Gītā*

Commentators on the *Gītā* differ amongst themselves in interpreting the meaning of the term *akṣara*. Śaṅkara takes *akṣara* here as contrary of *kṣara* (perishable). It is *Māyā-śakti*, (*akṣara*$_2$), the illusion power of the Lord. It is "the germ from which the perishable being takes its birth, the seat of all latent impressions (*saṁskāras*) of desires, action, etc., pertaining to the numerous mortal creatures.[122]

> The imperishable is what is known as immutable (*Kūṭastha*) ...that which remains immovable like a heap. Or, *kūṭa* means illusion, and *kūṭastha* means that which manifests itself in various forms of illusion and deception.[123]

For Śaṅkara the *akṣara* is *Kūṭastha Puruṣa*. It is unchangeable. It is the *māya-śakti* of the Lord which is eternal. It is 'unshakable' for Śaṅkara.

119 Swami Gambhirananda, *Brahma-Sūtra-Bhāṣya*, p. 659

120 *Ibid.*, p. 833.

121 *Śaṅkarabhāṣya*, Gītā Press, p. 363.

122 A. Mahadeva Sastri., *The BGB*, V. Ramaswamy Sastrulu & Sons, Madras, 1947, p. 410.

123 *Ibid.*, p. 410.

But sometimes *akṣara* *(akṣara$_1$)* has been taken as the *nirguṇa* Brahman. While discussing the two types of worshipers...the worshipper of *akṣara* and the worshipper of *Puruṣa*, Arjuna asks which is superior ?

> Those devotees who, always devout, thus contemplate Thee, and those also who (contemplate) the Imperishable, the Unmanifest,... which of them are better versed in *Yoga* ?[124]

Here, the Imperishable *(akṣara)* is unmanifest *(avyakta)* i.e., incomprehensible to the senses, writes Śaṅkara. It is devoid of all conditions *(upādhis)*. It can't be difined by words. It is unthinkable, invisible and unchangeable. Therefore it is said :

> Those who ever contamplate the Imperishable, the Indefinable, the Unmanifest, the Omnipresent and the Unthinkable, the Unchangeable, the Immutable, the Eternal...having restrained all the senses, always equanimous, intent on the welfare of all beings,...they reach Myself.[125]

The Imperishable which is the object of contemplation *(upāsanā)* is thus qualified. It is to be noted that *Kūṭastha Puruṣa* may mean *māyā-śakti* or *Īśvāra* who exerts the *māyā-śakti*. Śaṅkara explains :

> *Kūṭa* means a thing which is good to all appearance but evil within. Accordingly it refers here to the seed of *saṁsāra* ...including *avidyā* (nescience) and other things,...which is full of evil within, designated by various terms such as *Māyā*, *Avyākṛita* (undifferentiated) (*ŚU* IV.10), and in the *Gītā* (VII.14) *Kūṭastha* means He who is seated in *Māyā* as Its Witness, as its Lord. Or, *Kūṭastha* may mean 'remaining like a heap'.[126]

Thus, *akṣara* in this sense is *Īśvara*. This *kūṭastha-akṣara* can be taken as the *akṣara$_4$*. This explanation of Śaṅkara rightly corresponds to the nature of the description of the

124 A. Mahadeva Sastri, *The BGB*, V. Ramaswamy Sastrulu & Sons, Madras, 1947, p. 302.

125 *Ibid.*, p. 304.

126 *Ibid.*, p. 305.

Aśvattha tree in relation to the creation of this universe in the 15th discourse of the *Gītā*. While discussing the nature of the indestructible *Aśvattha*, Śaṅkara writes that Brahman with *Māyā* is the cause. He is eternal, as He is great. He is spoken of as the one above. "The One above is the root of this Tree of *Saṁsāra*".[127]

This unmanifested *Akṣara* is the Goal. It is very difficult for the embodied to reach at this Goal, says the *Gītā*. In the 15th discourse it has been further stated that out of two beings in the world...the perishable *(kṣara)* and the imperishable *(akṣara)* :

> The perishable comprises all creatures, the immutable is called the imperishable.[128]

The imperishable, the seed of *saṁsāra* does not perish so long we are under the spell of ignorance. In the 18th *śloka* of the same chapter the Lord says :

> I am higher than the perishable, the Tree of illusory *Saṁsāra*, called *Aśvattha* and the imperishable, the seed of that Tree of *Saṁsāra*.[129]

This *Kūṭastha Prakṛti*, (the *Māyā-śakti* of the Lord) comprising three *guṇas* is the material cause of this universe, says the *Gītā*.

> My womb is the great Brahman; in that I place the germ; thence, O Bharata, is the birth of all beings.[130]

Śaṅkara writes that the *Kūṭastha Prakṛti* i.e., the inferior and superior Nature is the source and the energy of all modifications. It is the *Mahad Brahma*. The Lord says 'The deluded world knows not Me, unborn and imperishable' (*BGB* VII. 24) because of the *Yoga-māyā*. From this unmanifested *akṣara*, all the manifestation...all creatures moving and unmoving come into being at the coming on of day and they disolve into it at

127 A. Mahadeva Sastri, *The BGB*, V. Ramaswamy Sastrulu & Sons, Madras, 1947, p. 397.

128 *Ibid.*, p. 410.

129 *Ibid.*, p. 411.

130 *Ibid.*, p. 380.

the coming on of night.[131] This *avyakta* (*akṣara*) is *Avdiyā*...the seed of all the created beings. All beings dwell in It. They are under the control of the *Prakṛti* i.e., of *Avidyā* (IX.7-8). Interpreting the 10th *śloka* of the 9th chapter of the *Gītā*, Śaṅkara writies that 'My *Māyā* i.e., the *Avidyā*, composed of the three *guṇas*, produces the universe comprising the moving and the unmoving objects'.[132]

In certain passages of the *Gītā*, *akṣara* is designated as *nirguṇa* Brahman and this is identified with the self. It is immutable *(avikriya)*.

> Whoever looks upon Him as the slayer, and whoever looks upon Him as the slain, both these know not aright. He slays not, nor is He slain [133]
>
> He is not born, nor does He ever die; after having been, He again ceases not to be; nor the reverse. Unborn, eternal, unchangeable and primeval, He is not slain when the body is slain.[134]

Thus, this Self is unchangeable, partless and devoid of qualities and 'the *Veda* comes from the Imperishable *akṣara*, the Highest Self.'[135] The Supreme Brahman is the Imperishable (*akṣara*) '*akṣaraṁ brahma paraman*'. The *Sruti* says, 'The Imperishable, as the *brahmaṇe* declare, not gross, not subtle' etc., (*BU* III 8.8). It is devoid of all attributes...*na kṣarati iti akṣaram. Akṣara* is the *para* Brahman, the Supreme Being. 'He does not perish when all beings perish'. That's why the *Gītā* says :

> Thou art the Imperishable, the Supreme Being worth to be known. Thou art the Great Abode of this Universe; Thou art the undying Guardian of the Eternal *Dharma*, Thou art the ancient *Puruṣa*.[136]

131 A. Mahadeva Sastri, *The BGB*, V. Ramaswamy Sastrulu & Sons, Madras, 1947, p. 231.

132 *Ibid.*, p. 244.

133 *Ibid.*, p. 40.

134 *Ibid.*, p. 41.

135 *Ibid.*, p. 101.

136 *Ibid.*, p. 283.

Śaṅkara interprets here the term *akṣara* as the *Paramātmā*, the Supreme Brahman (VIII. 3) which is indestructible. It is the highest goal (VIII. 21). It is beyond both the *sat* and the *asat*. It is the Lord of the Lords, the Abode of the Universe (XI. 37).

Akṣara is also taken as *Praṇavaḥ* in the *Gītā* (*akṣara*$_3$). The Lord himself says 'I am the syllable *Om* in all the *Vedas*', sound in ether, humanity in men.[137] The *Śruti* passages describe the syllable *Om* either as an expression of the *para* Brahman or as a symbol of Him. It is meant for the persons of dull and middling intellect, says Śaṅkara. In the 9th and 11th *ślokas* of the 8th chapter of the *Gītā*, *Om* is used as a means of knowing the *para* Brahman.

> Having closed all the gates, having confined mind in the heart, having fixed his life-breath in the head, engaged in firm *Yoga*, uttering Brahman, the one-syllabled *Om* thinking of Me, who departs, leaving the body, he reaches the Supreme Goal.[138]

Besides the three meanings in the *Gītā* we find *akṣara* also being used as *Īśvara* in the fourth sense indicated before. The Highest *Puruṣa* (*Īśvara*) by whom the whole world is pervaded and in whom all beings dwell is to be attained by exclusive devotion, says Śaṅkara.[139]

Thus, in the *Gītā* we find the term *akṣara* sometimes is taken as the Supreme Self, devoid of all conditions (*upādhis*) and sometimes is taught as the Lord of the Universe having the *upādhis* which is the cause of this Universe. In the 11th discourse, this *Īśvara* aspect of *Akṣara* has been discussed which manifests the whole universe. That's why the Lord says :

> Those who, fixing their thought on Me, contemplate Me, always devout, endued with supreme faith, those in my opinion are the best *Yogins*.[140]

137 A. Mahadeva Sastri, *The BGB*, V. Ramaswamy Sastrulu & Sons, Madras, 1947, p. 211.

138 *Ibid.*, p. 229.

139 *Ibid.*, p. 233.

139 *Ibid.*, p. 233.

140 *Ibid.*, p. 303.

Though described as Imperishable, the Supreme, this Brahman has been taken to be *Īśvara* by Śaṅkara as he brings in His relationship with this world. Thus, *akṣara*, is to be construed as *Īṣvara* the Lord of the Universe, when it is associated with adjuncts (*upādhis*). In the 37th *śloka* of the 11th chapter and 3rd *śloka* of the 12th chapter *Īśvara* is indicated by the term *akṣara*.

> But those who worship Me, renouncing all actions in Me, regarding Me Supreme, meditating on Me with exclusive devotion...I become the deliverer out of the Ocean of the mortal *saṁsāra*.[141]

Thus, this *akṣara Puruṣa* is designated as *Īśvara* in the *Gītā*. 'It dwells in the hearts of all beings, whirling by *Māyī* all beings (as if) mounted on a machine' (XVII. 61). This is called the *Puruṣottama uttamaḥ puruṣaḥ* of the *Gītā*. In the world as well as in the *Veda* the *Puruṣottama* is regarded as 'the Highest Spirit' (XV. 18).

Notes to Chapter III :

*Mr. P.M. Modi in his book, *Akṣara—A Forgotten Chapter in the History of Indian Philosophy* has raised certain points of doubt regarding the concept *akṣara*. Quoting passages from the *Upaniṣads* he writes :

> *Akṣara* is the matrix, *yoni* in respect to *puruṣa* (*MU* III.i.3b) and that "the male pours seed into the female" (*MU* II.i.5). The *ŚU* confirms this idea of the relation (*SU* I.2, VI.16a, V. 6) but explains it further : *akṣara* is a power of the Lord (*ŚU* III. 3), an unborn female (I. 9) ; *akṣara* is the *māyā* or *prakṛti* and *puruṣra* is the *māyīn*, the possessor of *māyā* (IV. 10); *akṣara* is "the ruled" and *puruṣa* is "the ruler" (*ŚU* I.B) ...*akṣara* is the *dharma*, *puruṣa* is the *dharmin*'.

(Quoted from *Akṣara-A Forgotten Chapter*, printed at Baroda State Press, Baroda, 1932, p. 14).

Nowhere Mr. Modi has attempted to trace out the different categories of *akṣara*. As a result of which the whole concept *akṣara* seems to be most confusing. But if we take $akṣara_1$ as 'the Supreme Brahman', and $akṣara_2$ as 'the lower Brahman',

141 A. Mahadeva Sastri, *The BGB*, V. Ramaswamy Sastrulu & Sons, Madras, 1947, p. 306.

then there would be no difficulty in understanding the different language games played by the upaniṣadic *sūtrakāras* in connection with this much discussed concept. Mr. Modi is often at a loss to explain how the personal (*puruṣa*) must be higher than the impersonal (*akṣara*). *Akṣara*, besides meaning Brahman also means *kūṭastha-māyā-śakti*. So it is under the control of *Puruṣa* or *Īśvara*. Mr. Modi writes that "*Akṣara* is neither identified with *puruṣa* nor it is lower than *puruṣa*. Each by itself is the highest object of human life." (Quoted from Mr. P. M Modi's book *Akṣara—A Forgotten chapter*, p. 12).

But once the distinction is made as I have done, difficulty no more remains as one may worship *saguṇa* Brahman as the highest which is taken as *Puruṣa* or the *nirguṇa* Brahman which is taken as *Akṣara*. I shall discuss this point in my *Puruṣottama* chapter in detail.

CHAPTER VI

PURUṢOTTAMA

1. TAJJALĀN

(A) Maheśvara

In Section One of the last chapter, I have discussed in detail the concept of *akṣara* found in the *Upaniṣads* which has been taken in the light of Brahman (*akṣara*$_1$), *Māyā-śakti* (*akṣara*$_2$), *Praṇava* (*akṣara*$_3$) and *Īśvara* (*akṣara*$_4$). I have pointed out how there is a good deal of differences between these four *akṣara-puruṣas*.

In the *Gītā*, one comes across a passage which discusses the nature of the triple *Puruṣas*[1]—the *kṣara*, the *akṣara* and the *puruṣottama*. The *Puruṣottama*, the *Uttamaḥ Puruṣaḥ*, is beyond both the *kṣara* and the *akṣara* (*kṣaraś cākṣara eva ca*). This *Uttamaḥ Puruṣaḥ* of the *Gītā* represents the *saguṇa* Brahman (*Īśvara*) of the *Upaniṣads* and the *Branma-Sūtra*, and the *Puruṣottama* of the *Purāṣas* and the *Vṣhṇusahasranāma*. The *Puruṣottama* differs from the *kṣara puruṣa* on the one hand and the *kūṭastha-akṣara* on the other hand. The *kūṭastha-akṣara* has been understood as the *māyā-śakti* which conditions everything by names and forms and attributes. Its two powers are the concealment (*āvaraṇa*) and projection (*vikṣepa*). The *māyā-śakti* can be viewed in three ways—the creation (*sṛṣṭi*), sustenance (*sthiti*) and dissolution (*pralaya*) of the world. This *Puruṣottama* is both transcendent and immanent in nature. It is

1 A. Mahadevi Sastri, *The BGB*, V. Ramaswamy Sastrulu & Sons, Madras, 1947, p. 411.

both the *kṣara* and the *akṣara* and again it is beyond both, over and above all mundane existence (*ekāṁseno sthitojagat*). The *Gītā's Puruṣottama* is almost identical with the upaniṣadic *Īśvara*.

The upaniṣadic *Īśvara* is the *apara* Brahman of Śaṅkara. The *apara* Brahman is the material as well as the efficient cause of the universe. This *apara* Brahman is expressed through the word *tajjalān*.[2] Śaṅkara explains that the term *tajjalān* incorporates three words in it—viz., *tajjam, tallam* and *tadana*. '*Tad*' should be read with each one of them. Śaṅkara further writes, *tajjam* signifies that this Universe comes forth from Brahman, *tallam* implies that, in the Brahman the universe will merge, and *tadana* expresses that in the Brahman, the Universe lives, moves and have its beings. Thus, the term *tajjalān* implies that the Brahman is immanent in the whole manifested universe. This Brahman is all-pervasive like space (*ākāśātmā*) and of the nature of pure intelligence (*bhārūpa*). He is the store-house of all desires (*sarvakāma*), all odours (*sarvagandha*), and all tastes (*sarvarasa*).[3]

The *AiU* accepts the existence of this self (*ātmā ekaḥ eva*) alone which is all-pervasive, omnipresent, eternal, pure consciousness, free, birthless, immortal, undecaying, fearless and one without a second[4] and the Supreme Deity is to be realised as the Self of one's own as also of all beings. It is the source of the origination, continuance and dissolution of the world. It identifies Himself with the individual souls by entering into its body for self-realisation. Thus, the Lord Supreme exists in all the bodies. The individual soul realises this *Puruṣa* (*etam eva puruṣam*) as the Lord of creation etc., as the Brahman, the Great.[5] He is not only Brahman, the inferior or (*Hiraṇyagarbha*) but also the vital force (*prāṇa*, possessing power of action) and

2 S. Radhakrishnan, *The Principal Upaniṣads*, George Allen & Unwin Ltd., London, 1953, p. 391.

3 *Ibid.*, p. 391.

4 Swami Gambhirananda, *Eight Upaniṣads*, Vol. II, Advaita Ashrama, Calcutta, 1972, p. 20.

5 *Ibid.*, p. 43.

also the conscious soul existing in all the bodies. "This is *Indra*, this is *Prajāpati*, this is all these Gods, etc." (*AiU* III.i.3). He is the *Antaryāmin* (the Inner Controller). The nature of the *antaryāmin* has been discussed in the *BU* wherein Yājñavalkya says to Uddālaka Āruṇi :

> He who dwells in (cosmic forces) the earth, the water, the fire, the sky, the air, the heaven, the sun, the quarters, the moon, the stars, the ether, the darkness and the light, etc., and in beings (and in bodily forces), such as the breath, the organ of speech, the eye, the ear, the mind, the skin, etc., (ranging from *Brahmā* to a clump of grass), yet is within them, whom they do not know, whose body they are, who controls them from within, He is your Ātman, the inner controller, the immortal (*BU* III.7.3 to 23).[6]

It is that Entity which appears many under different names and forms and is thought of differently by all creatures as well as the logicians.[7] The different creatures, having different names and forms under the spell of limiting adjuncts originate from that Immutable and into that very Immutable, they merge again at the time of dissolution of the bodies.[8] This Immutable is the indwelling Self of all the creatures of the three worlds (*sarvabhūtāntarātmā*). That which is bright and is subtler than the subtle, and that on which are fixed all the worlds as well as the dwellers of the worlds, is this Immutable Brahman. 'It is this vital force, It again is speech and mind' (*MU* II.ii.2). One must fix one's mind on this Immutable for It is true (*satya*), immortal (*amṛtam*). That Self which is *sarvajña* (all-knower), and *sarvavit* which is seated in the space within the luminous city of Brahman is conditioned by mind (*manomaya*). In the *MU*, we come across the descriptions of two birds clinging to the tree (subtle body) out of which 'one eats the fruit and the other one looks on without eating'.[9] That one which enjoys the divergent tastes of the fruit is the *Jivātman* being encaged by

6 S. Radhakrishnan, *The Principal Upaniṣads*, pp. 225-30.
7 Swami Gambhirananda, *Eight Upaniṣads*, Vol II, p. 74.
8 *Ibid.*, p. 113.
9 *Ibid.*, p. 143.

the limiting adjuncts. And the bird which simply looks on without tasting the fruit is *Īśvara* who is by nature eternal, pure, wise and free, who is omniscient and has the totality of *Māyā* as His limiting adjuncts. This *Īśvara* simply observes (*abhicākasīti*) the enjoyer and the enjoyed, writes Śaṅkara.[10]

The *Īśvara* is supramundane, is the Lord of the universe, not affected by the hunger, thirst, sorrow, death and delusion. The Supreme Lord under discussion is "the Vital Force of the vital forces, shines divergently through all beings (*sarvabhūtaiḥ*) from *Brahmā* to a clump of grass."[11] *Īśvara* thus is the creator of this world and this world is superimposed on Him. The *MU* (II.ii.11) writes that one attains the God who is everywhere, before and behind, to the right and to the left, above and below looks upon the world as the best of all possible worlds.[12] We find a similarity between the description of the cosmic God in the *MU* and the description of the *Viśvarūpa* in the 11th chapter of the *Gītā*. The cosmic God is the Supreme Ruler and Supreme Self of all beings and He rules all-moving and non-moving, beings. "He is all-pervasive, pure, bodiless (*akāya*), without wound (*avraṇam*), without sniews, taintless, untouched by sin, omniscient, ruler of mind, transcendent and self-existent".[13] This Omniscient God is worshipped through meditation. "He who knows these two—the Unmanifested and Destruction (*Hiraṇyagarbha*)—together, attains immortality through the the Unmanifested by crossing death througth Destruction"[14].

The *Hiraṇyagarbha* (*sūtrātmā*) is the end of all desires (*MU* III.ii.2). It is the support of the world (*jagataḥ pratiṣṭhā*) because of his all-pervasiveness, comprising all that is personal, elemental, heavenly, etc. One must meditate on It through *Adhyātma-Yoga* (*KU* I.ii.11). The *Hiraṇyagarbha* (*mahānātmā*) is higher than the intellect. It consists of both intelligence and activity (*KU* I.iii.10). This God is in the solar Orb. The face

10 Swami Gambhirananda, *Eight Upaniṣads*, Vol. II, p. 145.
11 *Ibid.*, p. 148.
12 *Ibid.*, p. 142.
13 Swami Gambhirananda, *Eight Upaniṣads*, Vol. I, p. 14.
14 *Ibid.*, p. 22.

of this Lord is concealed with a golden vessel (*Hirṇamayeṇ pātreṇa*).[15] The Lord is to be worshipped (*upāsitavyam*) by all creatures, since It is the indwelling Self. This Self is to be realised through hearing (*śravaṇa*), thinking (*manana*) and meditation (*nididhyāsana*) by a desireless man, says Śaṅkara.

> Having meditated on the Self, as bodiless in the midst of bodies, as permanent in the midst of the impermanent, and as great and pervasive, the wise man does not grieve.[16]

A man having discriminating intellect and a controlled mind attains the *paramam padam*, the highest place (figuratively) of *Viṣṇu*—"of the all-pervading Brahman,[17] of the supreme Self who is called *Vāsudeva*." This Supreme Self, the *Puruṣottama* who is hidden in all beings (*sarveṣu bhūtṣeu*) is covered by *Māyā* (cosmic illusion). The *smṛti* says, 'I am not revealed to all being veiled by my *Yoga-māyā*, etc. (*BGB* VII.25). The Lord who is essentially a mass of pure consciousness, is devoid of all worldly attributes, is the supporter of life etc., and is the Lord of the past and the future and apprears diversely being endowed with the limiting adjuncts.

The *KU* further adds that this *Puruṣa*, which is of the size of a thumb (*aṇguṣṭhamātraḥ*) resides in the body, is the ruler of the past and future, is enternal, unchanging, exists now in all beings and will even exist tomorrow. It (*sarvabhūtāntarātmā*) assumes different forms (*rūpaṁ rūpaṁ pratirūpaḥ*) as per the shapes of the individual and yet it is outside just like fire and wind manifest different forms and shapes in the world.[18] And in this way, the author of the *KU* arrives at the conception of the simultaneous immanence and transcendence of the Universal Spirit. The Universal Spirit, which from one point of view may be regarded as God (*Puruṣottama*) and from another point of view as the Absolute (*nirguṇa* Brahman), takes on both personal and impersonal shapes, inasmuch as it essentially transcends

15 Swami Gambhirananda, *Eight Upaniṣads*, Vol. I, Advaita Ashrama, Calcutta, p. 24.

16 *Ibid.*, p. 147.

17 *Ibid.*, p. 159.

18 *Ibid.*, p. 192.

them both.[19] This Self is not affected by the sorrows of the world (*na lipyate lokaduḥkhena*). From 9th to 15th *ślokas* of the Canto II, Part II of the *KU*, there is the discussion about the nature of the Supreme Lord (*Puruṣottama*). In the *KU*, we also note the description of *Aśvattha* tree like the *Gītā* which is compared with the universe having its roots above—the root being the abode of the Supreme *Viṣṇu*, the creator, sustainer and destroyer of this world.[20] This Universe emerges and moves becouse there is the Supreme Brahman,[21] ever seated in the hearts of all beings, one should separate this Self from one's body like a stalk from the *Muñja-grass*,[22] writes Śaṅkara.

The nature of this Self, the Highest Reality (*Puruṣottama*) has been discussed vividly from 1st *śloka* to 4th *śloka* and again from 7th *śloka* to 21st *śloka* of the 3rd chapter of the *ŚU*.

> Higher than this is Brahman, the supreme, the great hidden in all creatures according to their bodies, the one who envelopes the Universe, knowing Him, the Lord, (men) become immortal.[23]

The reference here is to *Īśvara* who is higher than the *Hiraṇyagarbha* and *Virāṭ-rūpa*, to the indwelling Lord, *antaryāmin*, to the Supreme Personal God, *Parameśvara*, writes Radhakrishnan.[24] This Lord is the Omnipresent *Śiva* (*tasmāt sarvagataś śivah*), the Primeval, Supreme *Puruṣa* (*puruṣaṁ mahāntam*), interpretes Śaṅkara. The Supreme *Puruṣa* creates this world through his power of *māyā*, *dsvātma-śakti* (*māyī sṛjati viśvam*). The ātman is bound in the absence of the Lord (*īśa*) since he is the enjoyer. One who knows this '*īśa*' (*deva*), is free from all fetters and thus 'attains immortality.'[25] Like the *Gītā*, the *ŚU*

19 S. Belvalkar and R. D. Ranade, *History of Indian Philosophy, the Creative Period*, Oriental Book Reprint Corporation, New Delhi, 1974, p 266.

20 Swami Gambhirananda, *Eight Upaniṣads*, Vol. I, p. 199.

21 *Ibid.*, p. 202.

22 *Ibid*, p. 216.

23 S. Radhakrishnan, *The Principal Upaniṣads*, George Allen & Unwin Ltd., London, 1953, p. 727.

24 *Ibid.*, p. 727.

25 *Ibid.*, p. 714.

also says that over both the *kṣara* (perishable) and the *akṣara* (imperishable), the one God (*deva*) rules who is the creator and the ruler. By meditating on Him, one can be free from illusion (*māyānivṛttiḥ*).[26] He is present in the Self (*ātmasaṁstha*). There is nothing higher than this Lord. This Great Primeval *Puruṣa* is smaller than small, greater than great, is hidden in the heart of the creature (*ŚU* III.20). The Great Lord (*maheśvara*) is the illusion-maker (*māyīn*),[27] 'in whom this whole world comes together and dissolves (*ŚU* IV.11), is the creator and supporter of the Gods, the ruler of all' (IV.12). He is the supreme Mighty Lord (*maheśvara*) of Lords, the supreme Divinity of divinities, the supreme Ruler of rulers. He is thus 'the Lord of the world, the adorable God'[28] (*paramaṁ maheśvaram*). He is the ruler of Primary Matter (*Pradhāna*), and of the spirit (*kṣetrajña*), the Lord of qualities (*guṇas*). He is hidden in all beings (*sarva-bhūteṣu*), all-pervading (*sarvavyāpin*) and the inner self of all being (*sarva-bhūtāntar-ātmā*).[29]

(B) Dahara Puruṣa

In the *CU*, it has been asked to worship this '*dahara puruṣa*' which implies the meditation of one's self as the Reality existing in the heart...'*ayaṁ vāva sa yo' yaṁ antar-hṛdaya ākāśaḥ, tad etat pūrṇam aparavarti.*'

> That which is (designated as) Brahman, even that is this *Ākāśa* outside the body. That which is the *ākāśa* outside the body, even that is the *ākāśa* inside the body. That which is the *ākāśa* inside the body even that is the *Ākāśa* within the lotus of the heart. This Brahman is all feeling and unchanging.[30]

Śaṅkara explains this point further. The concept *ākāśa* though one, it is divided into three different parts relating to

26 S. Radhakrishnan, *The Principal Upaniṣads*, George Allen and Unwin Ltd., London, 1953, p. 715.

27 *Ibid.*, p. 734.

28 *Ibid.*, p. 745.

29 *Ibid.*, p. 746.

30 *Ibid.*, p. 388.

the waking, dream and deep sleep states of the human life on these basis of the varieties of experiences. Out of all these, the deep sleep state is the most perfect state, wherein, one feels absolute happiness free from all pain. This is the supreme place says Śaṅkara and the *Puruṣa* which is lodged inside this *ākāśa* of the heart is unchanging and imperishable.

> This *Puruṣa* within the heart, smaller than a grain of rice, than a barley corn, than a mustard seed, than a grain of a millet. This is myself within the heart, greater than the earth, greater than the atmosphere, greater than the sky, greater than these worlds.[31]

The *CU* recommends primarily two types of meditations—with regard to body *(adhyātma)* and with regard to God *(adhidaivata)*.[32] The *Adhidaivata* Brahman is called *ākāśa*. *Ākāśa* is used here as it is "all-pervading, subtle and free from limitations", writes Śaṅkara. The lotus of the heart is the place of the Manifest Brahman. It manifests the world of names and forms dwelling there as a *Jīva*.

> Now, here in this city of Brahman is an abode, a small lotus flower; within it is a small space. What is within that should be sought, for that, assuredly, is what one should desire to understand.[33]

The body of the man is taken as the abode of Brahman *(brahmapura)*. The space *(daharam)* within the lotus-like chamber *(puṇḍarīka-sadṛśam)* of the heart stands for Brahman, interprets Śaṅkara. "The space within the heart consists of both heaven and earth, both fire and air, both sun and moon, lightning and the starts" (*CU* VIII.i.3). The space within the heart is not affected by the conditions of the body such as, old age, death and disease, etc., All desires are contained in it. It is the Self free from old age, sin, death. sorrow, hunger aud thirst, 'whose desire is the real, whose thought is the real.'[34] Thus, all

31 S. Radhakrishnan, *The Principal Upaniṣads*, George Allen and Unwin Ltd., London, 1953, pp. 391-92.

32 *Ibid.*, p. 397.

33 *Ibid.*, p. 491.

34 *Ibid.*, p. 492.

desires find their fulfilment in the self. The city of Brahman is within one's heart where we can possess all our desires. 'We daily get into the *Brahmā*-world while we are asleep', writes Śaṅkara.[35] "That self is (abides) in the heart. Therefore, it is the heart."[36] One has to realise the self in one's heart. One realises the true nature of the self within the space of the heart in the deep sleep state. This is called the Ātman, the immortal, the fearless.[37] The troubles of the world stands no longer in the *Brahmā*-world. One having disciplined life possesses that *Brahmā*-world.[38]

One should meditate on that being completely detached from the external world. The *KU* declares that this Supreme *Puruṣa* which is of the size of thumb dwells in the cavity of the heart.[39] Although he appears to be dwelling in the heart and animating all the senses and mind, yet He transcends all of them. He the final substratum and the highest goal *(sā kāṣṭhā sā parā gatiḥ)*.[40] He resides in the city (of the heart)...*'saḥ ahaṁ asmi'*—"that person am I."[41]

One who knows this *Puruṣa*, as existing in the heart, destroys the knot of ignorance (*MU* II.i.10). This *Jyotirmaya Puruṣa* (golden hued), which exists in the lotus of the heart inside the body is attainable through truth, constant meditation, complete knowledge *(samyag-jñāna)* and continuance *(brahma-caryeṇa)*.[42] This *Puruṣa* is all-pervasive, self-effulgent. It is seated in the very body, in the cavity of the heart.[43] This *Puruṣa* is not attained through the study of the *Vedas* and scriptures, nor through the intellect, nor through hearing. It is ever attained.[44]

35 S. Radhakrishnan, *The Principal Upaniṣads*, George Allen & Unwin Ltd., London, 1953, p. 715.

36 *Ibid.*, p. 496.

37 *Ibid.*, p. 496.

38 *Ibid.*, p. 497.

39 Swami Gambhirananda, *Eight Upaniṣads*, Advaita Ashrama, Calcutta, 1972, Vol. I, p. 181.

40 *Ibid.*, p. 160-61.

41 *Ibid.*, p. 25.

42 *Ibid.*, Vol. II, p. 151.

43 *Ibid.*, p. 154.

44 *Ibid.*, p. 161.

The *MāU* asserts this point further by stating that the Supreme Reality which is called *Prajāpati*, *Rudra*, *Śiva* and *Nārāyaṇa* is all-pervasive residing in the space of heart *hṛdayākāśa* or *dahara*) as an intelligent principle.[45]

The author of the *TU* further adds that the person who resides in the space within the heart is realised through knowledge, and thus is immortal and effulgent.[46] *Puruṣa* is (derivatively) so called because of sleeping (*śayana*) within '*puri*', the city (of the heart), writes Śaṅkara. All things are hidden in the cavity of the heart during creation, sustenance and dissolution of the world. The cosmic unmanifested (*Māyā*) itself in the cavity of the heart is the supreme space. From the above *śruti* passages, it follows that the self (Supreme Self, the *Puruṣottama*) is placed in the cavity of the intellect "which is the cause of Its experience," according to Śaṅkara. And the *śruti* passages like "Having created it, He entered into that very being" (*TU* II.vi) is a mere repetition of the same thought process. The Brahman, after creating the effect "has entered into the creation, is perceived within the cavity of the intellect as possessed of such distinctions as being a seer, a hearer, a thinker, a knower, etc."[47] The term '*hṛdy-ākāśa*' is taken as the principle of consciousness in the *BU* which is hidden in all things as a razor in its case or as fire in wood (I.iv.7).

Thus, *Iśvara* resides in the space within the heart. In other words, the *śruti* says :

> The heart is Brahman. The heart is the abode of all beings. It should be meditated upon as stability. *Hiraṇyagarbha* is the presiding deity of the heart.[48]

This *Hiraṇyagarbha* is the Supreme Self. He is the Lord of all, the ruler of all, and governs whatever there is (*BU* V.vi.1).

45 Baldev Raj Sharma, *The Concept of Ātman in the Principal Upaniṣad*, Dinesh Publications, New Delhi, 1972, p. 211.

46 Swami Gambhirananda, *Eight Upaniṣads*, Advaita Ashrama, Calcutta, 1972, Vol. I, p 249.

47 *Ibid.*, p. 338.

48 S. Radhakrishnan, *The Principal Upaniṣads*, George Allen and Unwin Ltd, 1953, p. 251.

This cosmic person dwells in the heart. He is all-pervading and the Omnipresent *Śiva*. He is the mighty Lord (*Prabhu*), not longer than a thumb, dwelling within, is perceived by the heart, the thought, the mind. They who know it become immortal, says the *śruti*.

2. *ĪŚVARA*

In the *Brahma-Sūtra*, one find the concept '*para* Brahman *Paramātman*' is repeatedly talked about in different aphorisms, sometimes in connection with *nirguṇa* Brahman (*akṣara*$_1$) and sometimes in connection with *Īśvara* or *saguna* Brahman (*akṣara*$_4$ or *Puruṣottama*). Śaṅkara, while interpreting the original *sūtras*, has mentioned the twofold nature of the *Paramātman*, the Supreme Self viz., the *saguṇa* (form) and the *nirguṇa* (formless) Brahman.[49]

The *saguṇa* aspect of the *Paramātman* refers to the *Gītā's* concept of *Puruṣottama* which otherwise is designated as *Īśvara*. *Īśvara*, endowed with His *māyā-śakti* creates this Universe and He is the *abhinnanimittopādāna* of the world.' That (is Brahman from which (are derived) the birth etc., of this (Universe)."[50] Śaṅkara explains that Brahman is the source from which the birth, continuance and dissolution of this manifested universe of name and form are derived. The *śruti* also supports this view. 'that from which all these beings take birth, that by which they live after being born, that towards which they proceed and into which they merge that is Brahman' (*TU* III.ii).

The Omniscient God who is the cause of the world 'is known from the scriptures'[51] because of '*samanvayāt*', the object of their fullest import. This is the all-pervasive entity which is unchangeable and into which all things enter as their ultimate limit, writes Śaṅkara.[52]

49 Swami Gambhirananda, *Brahma-Sūtra Bhāṣya*, Advaita Ashrama, Calcutta, 1972, p. 62.

50 *Ibid.*, p. 13.

51 *Ibid.*, p. 18.

52 *Ibid.*, p. 37.

The *KU* describes this *Puruṣa* as follows :

There is nothing higher than *Puruṣa*. He is the culmination, He is the highest goal (I.iii.11).

All the *Upaniṣads* declare that consciousness is the cause of the Universe. 'He has no master, no ruler...no originator, no ordainer' (*ŚU* VI.9). The all-powerful God who is a conscious entity is to be viewed from two standpoints: One, having the limiting adjuncts which is a modification of name and form and the other, devoid of all conditioning factors.[53] The former one is Brahman which is the cause of all modifications inclusive of the Blissful one.[54] 'The Being inside is God, His qualities having been taught.'[55] The God possesses substances and the qualities by the power of his own *Māyā* (*KU* III.9) and He is the person residing in the eye and the sun, interprets Śaṅkara. Thus the God is the internal ruler, neither *Pradhāna* (*BSB* I.ii.19) nor the embodied soul (*BSB* I.ii.20). The Internal Ruler is to be meditated on since the characteristics of that (Supreme Self) are spoken of.[56] Neither Sāṅkhya's insentient *Pradhāna* nor the embodied soul is the internal ruler.[57] This Supreme Self is *Vaiśvānara*.[58] Śaṅkara writes, 'since the Supreme Self is the self of all, It can very well be both *Puruṣa* and have residence within *Puruṣa*.[59] This Supreme Self does manifest out of favour for His worshippers (*BSB* I.ii.29). It is the *Puruṣa* of the size of a thumb[60]...the ruler of the past and the future. For the meditation of such a *puruṣa*, the qualities like '*satyasaṁkalpa*' '*sarvavyāpakatā*', '*sarvātmaktā*', '*sarvaśaktimāna*', etc., are required. These qualities are not endowed with the *Jīvātman* but with the *Puruṣottama*. "This Self is to be realised, heard of, reflected on, and profoundly meditated upon is the Supreme Self."[61]

53 Swami Gambhirananda, *Brahma-Sūtra Bhāṣya*, Advaita Ashrama, Calcutta, 1972, p. 62.

54 *Ibid.*, p. 77.

55 *Ibid.* p. 79.

56 *Ibid.*, p. 133.

57 *Ibid.*, p. 135-136.

58 *Ibid.*, p. 146-48.

59 *Ibid.*, p. 151.

60 *Ibid.*, p. 202.

61 *Ibid.*, p. 282.

The Supreme Self is regarded as the material as well as the efficient cause of the world (*BSB* I.iv.23), because He has a 'will to create'. Creation and dissolution are both possible because of Brahman.[62] 'That created Itself by Itself' (*TU* II.vii). It is the source, *yoni*, says the *upaniṣad*. 'The source of all beings which the wise perceive' (*MU* I.i.3).

From the different *śrutis*, *smṛtis* and *Purāṇas*, it has been proved that Supreme Brahman is the cause of this Universe. 'I am the origin and dissolution of the whole Universe' (*BGB* VII.6). The objection has been raised by the opponents, "Brahman can't be the cause of the Universe owing to the dissimilarity) in the nature of this Universe, and the fact of being so is known from the *Vedas*,"[63] which has been refuted by the *Sūtrakāra*.

God by nature is eternal, pure, intelligent, omniscient and omnipresent. "Name and form constitute the seeds of the world because of ignorance, ever associated with God and are mentioned in the *Vedas* and the *Smṛtis* as the power, called *Māyā* of the Lord" (*BSB* II.i.14). He is the Lord of all. He is the ruler of all beings. He is the protector of all beings' (*BU* IV.4.22).

The *Sūtrakāra*, quoting passages from the *upaniṣads*, says, "*sarvopetā ca taddarśanāt*"—'Deity is possessed of all powers'.[64] It is eternal consciousness by Its very Nature. 'It appears to exist as an individual soul owing to the association with limiting adjuncts.'[65] But this Lord is least affected by things that condition them.[66] An individual being suffers owing to the ignorance caused by its identity with the body. But *Īśvara* is free from this. Śaṅkara makes this point clear by pointing out that 'a part of God which is conjured up by nescience, condition by the intellect etc., and called an individual soul suffers pain, still God, the possessor of that part does not suffer.[67] This God

62 Swami Gambhirananda, *Brahma-Sūtra Bhāṣya*, Advaita Ashrama, Calcutta, 1972, p. 294.
63 *Ibid.*, p. 307.
64 *Ibid.*, p. 358.
65 *Ibid.*, p. 476.
66 *Ibid.*, p. 510.
67 *Ibid.*, p. 510-11.

through constant meditation creates everything and being by means of His indicatory marks, writes Śaṅkara. 'He who inhabits the earth, and who controls the earth from within (is the Internal Ruler), (*BU* III.vii.3). The Supreme Soul rules over the individual souls having their inferior limiting adjuncts interprets Śaṅkara.[68] The individual soul suffers in this world due to ignorance but the Supreme Soul has no suffering. This Supreme Self is the 'highest place'...'the end of the road', says the scripture. Both in the *śruti* and *smṛti*, we find a number of passages ascribing the *saguṇa* and *nirguṇa* aspect of the Brahman. He is both the *para* and *apara*. It is not due to any distinction of cause and effect or the limiting adjunct.[69] The *smṛti* boldly declares, 'one who knows me as the *Puruṣottama*, he is the all-knowner' (*BGB* 15.19). The *saguṇa* nature of the lord is not due to the limiting adjuncts but it is the very nature of the lord to be endowed with the qualities, says Śaṅkara.[70]

The *Puruṣottama* is to be worshipped. When It is in the causal state (*kāraṇāvasthā*), It possesses both its *parā* and *aparā prakṛti* as two powers (*śakti*). It is unmanifested at this stage being non-different (*abhinna*) but when it is in the effect stage (*kāryāvasthā*), the two powers are manifested by different name and form. Thus in the *śruti* we find the Brahman in the causal state is called *nirākāra* (formless) and when it is in the effect state it is called *sākāra* (form). The power of the Lord is non-different from the Lord just as '*prakāśa āśrayavat*', says the *Sūtrakāra*. These two *prakṛtis* of the Lord are the cause of this Universe (*BGB* 7.4, 5) which is discussed as the *kṣara* and *akṣara* in the *ŚU* (1.10) and *kṣetra* and *kṣetrajña* (*BGB* 13.1). Out of these two, there is a third category of *Puruṣa* called the '*Puruṣottama*' which is superior to them (*BGB* 15.17) and this *Puruṣa* is discussed in the *Veda* "as there is the mention of the embankment *(setu)*, measure *(unmāna)*, connection *(sambandha)*, and difference *(bheda)*"[71] (*BSB* III.ii.31). This *Puruṣa* differs

68 Swami Gambhirananda, *Brahma-Sūtra Bhāṣya*, Advaita Ashrama, Calcutta, 1997, p. 509.

69 *Ibid.*, p. 610-13.

70 *Śaṅkarabhāṣya*, Gītā Press, Gorakhpur, p. 259.

71 *Ibid.*, p. 633.

from the vedic description of the *Puruṣa* in the eye *(netrāntar-varttī)* or *Puruṣa* in the sun *(sūryamaṇḍalavarttī)*, writes Śaṅkara.[72]

The Supreme *Puruṣa* which possesses a set of qualities is to be meditated on as it is, there in the lotus of the heart. The different *śruti* and *smṛti* passages support this view. 'The two who have entered into the cavity (of the heart) are the individual self and the supreme self'....[73] The *Sūtrakāra* further writes, "The small space (*daharākāśa*) is Brahman, on account of the subsequent reasons."[74]

The Vedāntin says, 'the small space Itself is Brahman'. It is neither the the material space nor the individual soul. The body is the city of the Brahman. The small space which is referred to *Brahmaloka* is to be understood in the sense of Brahman alone, says Śaṅkara.[75]

> And owing to the fact of holding (the worlds) in place, (the small space must be God); for this glory is noticed (in other texts) as pertaining to Him.[76]

The *upaniṣad* also supports this view by stating that 'under the mighty rule of this Immutable O Gārgī, the sun and the moon are held in their positions' etc. (*BU* III.viii,9). From 14th to 21st *sūtra* of the third *pāda* of the First *Adhyāya*, the discussion has been made in relation to *dahara puruṣa*.[77] This *dahara puruṣa* is none else but the *Puruṣottama*, the Lord of all. It exists inside the small space. It is to be sought for, to be enquired.

Śaṅkara's interpretation of '*dahara ākāśa*' as Brahman is also ambiguous as it mentions of both the *saguṇa* and *nirguṇa* Brahman.[78] However, when one relates the Brahman to this

72 *Śaṅkarabhāṣya*, Gītā Press, Gorakhpur, p. 297.

73 Swami Gambhirananda, *Brahma-Sūtra-Bhāṣya*, Advaita Ashrama, Calcutta, 1972, p. 120.

74 *Ibid.*, p. 180.

75 *Ibid.*, p. 186.

76 *Ibid.*, p. 186.

77 *Ibid.*, p. 180-89.

78 *Śaṅkarabhāṣya*, p. 809.

body (*dahara ākāśa*), the world when there is talk of any limitation, then one is bound to point out logically the *saguṇa* Brahman.[79] Thus the Supreme Self is the '*parama maheśvara*', '*parama-pati*', '*parama-devatā*', because of '*patyādiśabdebhyaḥ*'.[80]

> This Supreme Self is not affected by the limitations of either the perishable, or the imperishable entities. He is the 'Highest Self'. He is the ensouling consciousness permeating through all beings. It is through the spirit of consciousness that the Supreme Self enters, permeats and sustains, through His essence, the three worlds, *Bhūḥ*, *Bhūvaḥ* and *Svaḥ*, He is imperishable, He is the Lord, He is named *Nārāyaṇa*, also called *Īśvara*, because He is (*īśanaśīla*) who controls the three worlds.[81]

3. VĀSUDEVA

Akṣara has been used in the *Gītā* in four different ways. Śaṅkara interprets this term sometimes as *Nirguṇa* Brahman ($akṣara_1$), *Kūṭastha-akṣara* ($akṣara_2$), *Praṇava* ($akṣara_3$) and sometimes as *Īśvara* ($akṣara_4$) who creates, sustains and destroys this world.

$Akṣara_4$ stands for *Īśvara* which is synonymous with the *Puruṣottama* in the *Gītā*. The *Gītā's Puruṣottama* is the Supreme Lord,[82] the presiding deity of this manifested Universe. He is unborn, imperishable and the Lord of all beings.[83] This God is Brahman caught in the meshes of *Māyā*. He is conditioned and limited. He is the '*karmādhyakṣa*'. He is '*māyāviśiṣṭa caitanya*'. God being *māyāviśiṣṭa*, is conditioned by the *upādhis* of *Māyā*, which are what Śaṅkara calls '*niratiśaya upādhis*', while the *upādhis* of the *Jīvas* are "*nihinopādhi*". *Īśvāra* thus is *nitya-nivṛtta—avidyā*...ever free from *Avidyā*.[84] The world which

79 Dr. K.P. Mishra's paper "A note on *Dahara ākāśa*" (unpublished).

80 *Śaṅkarabhāṣya*, p. 239.

81 G. Jhā, *Śaṅkara Vedānta*, Darbhanga Lectures Seriesi No. 1, 1939, p. 166.

82 A. Mahādeva Śāstrī, *The BGB*, V. Ramaswamy Śastrulu and Sons, Madras, 1947, p. 192.

83 *Ibid.*, p. 121.

84 S.G. Mudgal, *Advaita of Śaṅkara—A Reappraisal*, Motilal Banarsidass, Delhi, 1975, p. 17.

comprises of three qualities of *sattva*, *rajas* and *tamas*...is the product of the Supreme Lord by His own *Māyā*.[85] *Īśvāra* is *Āptakāma*. He creates this world in a sportive spirit—"*lokavattu līlākaivalyam*".

The *Gītā* says the Supreme Lord by means of His two-fold *Prakṛti*...the inferior and the superior Nature.. the *Kṣetra* (Matter) and *Kṣetrajña* (Spirit), the *Prakṛti* and *Puruṣa* creates this Universe and He is also the sustainer and destroyer of the same universe.[86]

> By me all this world is pervaded, My form Unmanifested. All beings dwell in me; and I do not dwell in them.[87]

All beings (both movable and immovable) dwell in *Īśvara* who is all-pervasive (*matsthāni sarvabhūtāni*). They come and go again and again at the end of a *kalpa* as per their *svabhāva* or Nature.[88] The nature of this Lord has been discussed in the 7th and 9th chapters of the *Gītā*.

> I am the Goal, the Sustainer, the Lord, the Witness, the Abode, the Shelter and the Friend, the Origin, Dissolution and Stay, the Treasure-house, the Seed imperishable.[89]

The Supreme Lord designated as *Vāsudeva* is the source of this world (*vāsudevaḥ sarvamiti*). The wise men knowing this worship Him as the Supreme Reality. "He is the Supreme Brahman, the Supreme Light, the Supreme Purifier, the Eternal, Divine *Puruṣa*, the Primal God, Unborn and Omnipresent."[90] The *Gītā* further states: "He is the *Puruṣa* Supreme, Source of beings, Lord of beings, God of Gods, Ruler of the world.[91] The Supreme *Purṣa* has been manifested in this Universe and this aspect of the Lord has been described from 19th to 41st *ślokas* of the 10th chapter of the *Gītā*.

85 A. Mahadeva Sastri, *The BGB*, V. Ramaswamy Sastrulu and Sons, Madras, 1947, p. 210.

86 *Ibid.*, p. 210.
87 *Ibid.*, p. 241.
88 *Ibid.*, p. 243.
89 *Ibid.*, p. 249.
90 *Ibid.*, p. 266.
91 *Ibid.*, p. 266.

The third *śloka* of the 11th chapter of the *Gītā* distinctly points out that *Īśvara* is *Puruṣottama*[92] (*īśvaram puruṣottamam*). The Universal Form of *Puruṣottama* is manifested as the Universe and this form has been described from 9th to 17th *ślokas* and again from 18th *śloka* to the end of the eleventh chapter of the *Gītā*.[93] The Lord who adores this from is the Supreme Goal (*paramā gatiḥ*). He is the Ancient *Puruṣa* (*puruṣaḥ purāṇaḥ*), the Supreme Abode of all. Śaṅkara interprets that He is 'the *Kṣetrajña* (XIII.2) who appears to be a *saṁsārīn* owing to a distinction in the *upādhis* set up by *avidyā*, in the same way that the *Ātman* or individual Self appears (by *avidyā*) to be identical with the physical body etc.'[94] By this identity, the real nature of either *Īśvara* or the matter does not change, writes Śaṅkara. *Īśvara* is *māyādhyakṣa*. *Māyā* is within His control. *Īśvara* is not affected by *saṁsāra*. Both the *saṁsāra* and *saṁsārī* are creatures of *avidyā*, interprets Śaṅkara. But the *saṁsārī* (*kṣetrajña*) is not affected by *avidyā*. The *Puruṣa* is 'the Spectator and Permitter, Supporter, Enjoyer, the Great Lord, and also the Supreme Self in this body.'[95]

He exists in all the living creatures (*sarveṣu bhūteṣu tiṣṭhati*). Thus, it follows from the nature of the case that the *Gītā* does not distinguish the two...the *Īśvara* and the *Kṣetrajña*. The Supreme *Puruṣa* (*Puruṣottama*) through His *Īśvara-śakti* manifests this Universe and hence He is the Brahman.

To come back to the original simile, *Aśvattha*, the Tree of *Saṁsāra*, or the Cosmic Tree has its beginning...has its roots. the thread of causality (*Karma vipāka prakriyā*) has to be traced back to God himself who is the *Puruṣottama*. God is the First cause... the roots of the *Aśvattha*. This is the 'Highest Goal' says the *Gītā*.

Then that Goal should be sought for, whither having gone

92 A. Mahadeva Sastri, *The BGB*, V. Ramaswamy Sastrulu & Sons. Madras, 1947, p. 278.

93 *Ibid.*, p. 280-83. 283-301.

94 *Ibid.*, p. 321.

95 *Ibid.*, p. 360.

> none return again. I seek refuge in that Primeval *Puruṣa* whence streamed forth the Ancient Current.[96]

It is from this Primeval *Puruṣa* (*Ādi-Puruṣa*), the uncaused cause...the Tree of the illusory *Saṁsāra* comes into being, writes Śaṅkara. The nature of the *Ādi-Puruṣa* is discussed in the 17th, 18th and 19th *ślokas* of the 15th chapter of the *Gītā*.

> But distinct is the Highest Spirit spoken of as the Supreme Self, the indestructible Lord who penetrates and sustains the three worlds.[97]
>
> Because I transcend the perishable and am even higher than the imperishable, therefore am I known in the world and in the *Veda* as '*Puruṣottama*', the Highest Spirit.[98]
>
> He who, undeluded, thus knows Me, the Highest Spirit, he, knowing all, worships Me with his whole being.[99]

The Highest Spirit is distinct from the *kṣara* (perishable) and *akṣara* (imperishable). He is superior to *kṣara puruṣa*, the physical body and He is the Inner Self manifesting the universe by His *Māyā-śakti*. Therefore, He is called as the Supreme Self. He transcends the '*Aśvattha*' (*kṣara*) and is higher than even the *akṣara*, the seed of that Tree, writes Śaṅkara.

Śaṅkara translates the key words *atītaḥ* as 'transcending' and *uttamaḥ* as 'more-excellent'.[100] The *Puruṣottama* is the Super-excellent, or the 'Most excellent.' It is *uttamaḥ* in comparision to the *kṣara puruṣa* on the one hand *akṣara puruṣa* on the other hand. The use of the word *atitaḥ* suggests that there is a categorical difference between the *kṣara* and the *Puruṣottama* (*kṣaraṁ puruṣaṁ atitaḥ*). The *Puruṣottama* thus is quite a distinct category of a higher order which can't be

96 A. Mahadeva Sastri, *The BGB* V. Ramaswamy Sastrulu & Sons, Madras, 1947, p. 400.

97 *Ibid.*, p. 410.

98 *Ibid.*, p. 411.

99 *Ibid.*, p. 412.

100 "Rāmānuja terms for '*atītaḥ*' and '*uttamḥ*' would agree with that of Tilak as he renders '*uttamaḥ*' as '*utkṛṣṭatamaḥ*'... super-excellent." (Quoted from *Gītābhāṣya* of Rāmānuja tr. by M.R. Sampatkumar, Vidyā Press, Madras, 1969).

equited with the *kṣara puruṣa*. Śaṅkara says, this visible cosmos (*kṣara*) is the *upādhis* (adjuncts) of the *Puruṣottama*. The gross body, the *Jīva* which is an integral portion of the Lord, manifests himself in this world (*jīvaloke jīvabhūtaḥ sanātanaḥ*). Śaṅkara interprets that it is an imaginary portion, not a real portion limited by the *upādhis*, set up by *avidyā*. In the 13th chapter of the *Gītā*, it has been said that the *Jīva* is not a portion of the Lord. It is identified with the Lord.

The *Puruṣottama* can't be *kūṭastha akṣara*. It is *uttamaḥ puruṣaḥ* (*akṣarād api ca uttamaḥ*) higher than the *kūṭastha akṣara* which contains the seed of the *Aśvattha* tree. Śaṅkara translates *akṣara* as '*Māyā-śakti*' the illusion power of *Īśvara* but not *Īśvara* and *uttamaḥ* as 'Super-excellent'. It is an independent object of meditation and a goal (XII. 1-2). It is the highest *Puruṣa* called the *Puruṣottama* and by this *Puruṣa*, the whole world is pervaded. It is the Great Lord of beings (IX.11).

> I am the source of all : from Me everything evolves; thus thinking the wise worship Me, endowed with contemplation.[101]

Thus the *Gītā* distinctly proves that the Supreme Lord (*Puruṣottama*), termed as *Vāsudeva* is the source of the whole world. It is the Supreme *Puruṣa*—the ruler of the world. The Lord desired to see His form as *Īśvara* (*Īśvaraṁ puruṣottamam*) (XI. 3). The Ancient *Puruṣa* (*puruṣaḥ purāṇaḥ*) is the Supreme Abode of all beings(XI.38). Anybody who worships the Lord by exclusive devotion (VIII· 22) in the Universal Form gets rid of this mortal '*saṁsāra*' (XII. 7), says the *Gītā*. "At the end of many births, the man of wisdom comes to me, (realising) that *Vāsudeva* is the all (*vāsudevaḥ sarvamiti*), he is the noble-souled (*Mahātman*), very hard to find."[102] The Supreme Lord is imperishable. It exists in all beings. It is different from the Unmanifested, the *kūṭastha akṣara* which is *avidyā*.

The 22nd *śloka* of the 8th chapter and the 18th *śloka* of the 15th chapter conclusively prove that the *akṣara puruṣa* is

101 A Mahadeva Sastri, *The BGB*, V. Ramaswamy Sastrulu & Sons, Madras, 1947, p. 263.

102 *Ibid.*, pp. 215-16.

lower than the *Puruṣottama*. The use of the word *paraḥ* (VIII.22) implies that the *Puruṣottama* is higher (*paraḥ*) than the *akṣara*. This *Puruṣottama* who is superior to *kṣara* and higher than *akṣara* is said to be the 'Self abiding in all beings, and all beings abiding in the Self' (*sarvabhūtastham ātmānam*) and again He is the *kūṭastha akṣara*, appearing in the unmanifested form to manifest this universe. Thus, *akṣara* is taken in the *Gītā* in the sense of (1) *avyakta*, unmanifested *Māyā-śakti* and (2) *kūṭastha*, the supporter of this manifested form, the witness to all activity. The *Puruṣottama* is both *kṣara* and *akṣara* and again it is beyond the both. In other words, both the *kṣara* and *akṣara* are the characteristics of the *Puruṣottama*. The *Puruṣottama* is only one having both 'a *prakṛti*-referent and a *puruṣa*-referent' and so it is not a *Puruṣa* in the same sense as the other.[103] He is the Brahman, the *Parameśvara* (XI.3, XIII.27), the *Paramātman* (VI.7, XIII.22, XV.17, III.22), The *Kṣetrajña* or *akṣara puruṣa* (XII.2) and the *Kūṭastha Īśvara* (XIII.26, XV.16).

The *Puruṣottama* is linked up with this mutable world through His *Vibhūti* and '*Avatāra*'. Śaṅkara translates *Vibhūti** as '*Vistara*'...'expansion'.[104] In otherwords, the term *Vibhūti* implies that one who does his *svadharma* and *svabhāva* of his own race rises above the common humanity to reach at the divine humanity. For the pre-eminence of that divine humanity one must discharge his duties perfectly. When the common humanity is at stake and the law and order is distorted the Lord

103 William Beidler., *The Vision of Self in Early Vedānta*, Motilal Banrasidass, 1975, p. 117.

104 *Ibid.*, p. 183,

* Rāmānuja translates it as '*aiśvaryam*'... Lordship over the mutable world (X.7). Radhakrishnan explains it as right feeling, real, faith, glory. Only the last term really fits the meaning. It is the lack of appreciation of this term as shown by Śaṅkara and Rāmānuja's *Bhāṣya* which presents these from overcoming the metaphysical incompleteness of *Puruṣottama*. In the text, there is clear indication of its meanings such as in the following verses:

Of *Vedas* I am *Sāmaveda*, I am *Vāsudeva* of the *devas* and of senses I am mind (*manaḥ*), I am of living beings the intelligence (*cetanā*) etc. (*BGB* X.22).

descends to the universe in the form of *Avatāra*,[105] to safeguard the world at large. "The description of the *Avatāra* given by Śaṅkara in his introduction to his commentary on the *Gītā* in which he uses the phrases '*dehavānīva, jāta iva ca*', embodied as it were, born as it were, is inspired by this verse. The Lord... controls His triple power of *māyā* and "manifests Himself", "as though embodied, as though born", in exactly the same way as He manifests the world, "in order to bless the world" (*lokānugrahaṁ kurvan lakṣyate*).[106] These two concepts are discussed in the *Gītā* in detail. The birth of the *Avatāra* is voluntary. It is *ātma-māyā*.

> It is the manifestation from above of that which we have to develop from below, it is the descent of God into that divine birth of the human being into which we mortal creatures must climb, it is the attracting divine example given by God to man in the very type and form and perfected model of human existence.[107]

These two concepts imply that *Puruṣottama* which is the Highest Reality in Indian Philosophical Literature is not other-wordly. It descends to save the earthly Brahman (*bhaumasya brāhmaṇasya*) which is the 'twofold Vedic religion of Works and Renunciation that maintains order in the universe'. Thus, the so-called charge of the western thinkers against Indian Philosophy in general as other-worldly is proved to be fictitious and baseless.

The *Puruṣottama* of the *Gītā* is the transpersonal-personality. It is the *abhinnanimittopādānakāraṇa* of this world. It is the cause of both *kṣara* and *akṣara puruṣa*. The *kṣara puruṣa* comprises of the gross body and its cause is the subtle *prakṛti*, the *akṣara puruṣa*. The *kṣara* and the *akṣara* both depend on the *Puruṣottama*, for it is the material as well as the efficient cause of the both. Brahman can't be the cause of *Puruṣottama*,

105 A. Mahadeva Sastri, *The BGB*, V. Ramaswamy Sastrulu & Sons, Madras, 1947. pp. 121-22.

106 A. G. K. Warrior, *God in Advaita*, Indian Institute of Advanced Study, Simla, 1977, p. 156.

107 Śrī Aurobindo, *Essays on the Gītā*, New York, 1950, p. 140.

since It is Uncrused Cause. Brahman is the *adhiṣṭhāna* of all these. Hence, the *Vivartavāda*, which Śaṅkara propounds is a cancellation of the theory of causality. Commenting on the *Gītā*, Śaṅkara writes, "There is no other cause besides the Supreme Lord for He alone is the cause of this Universe."[108]

In the *Gītā*, we come across two types of worships—the worship of *akṣara* and the worship of *puruṣa*. Some scholars are of opinion that there are two distinct types of worship in the *Gītā* and accordingly there are two tiers[109] or double-decker.[110] *Puruṣa* and *Akṣara* constitute two different tiers of worship propounded in the *Gīta: Akṣara* worship refers to the upper tier (attributeless Brahman) and the *Puruṣa* worship stands for the lower tier (*Īśvara*). But in fact, these are not two distinct tiers. There is no question of double-decker. It is only two aspects of the same Reality. *Puruṣa upāsanā* and *Akṣara upāsanā* are two separate ways of worship prescribed in the *Gītā* for the devotees to reach the same goal. They are not two goals, but two distinct ways of worship to reach at the same goal.

Thus, the *Gītā's Puruṣottama* seems to be identified with the upaniṣadic *Īśvara*. It is beyond the subjectivity and the objectivity, the higher and the lower categories. The *Puruṣottama* can't be divided into the personal and impersonal aspects, though there are passages in the *Gītā* to support this view. He is in fact, beyond all these, transcends all these. Thus, the nature of this *Puruṣottama* is adequately expressed in the following lines :

> O Lord, in my meditation I have attributed forms to Thee, who art formless. O Thou Teacher of the world, in singing my hymn I have, as it were, belied the truth that Thou art

108 A. Mahadeva Sastri, *BGB*, p. 210.

109 S. G. Mudgal, *Advaita of Śaṅkara—A Reappraisal*, Motilal Banarsidass, 1975 pp. 1-2.

110 Ninnian Smart, *Doctrine and Argument in Indian Philosophy*, George Allen and Unwin, London, 1964, p. 100.

By consequence Śaṅkara formulates a double-decker theory of the Holy Power.

indescribable. By going on pilgrimage, I have, so to say, denied Thy Omnipresence. O Lord of the Universe, pray forgive me for these threefold faults.[111]

111 C.P.R. Aiyer, "One Thread of Unity", Published in *Voice of Samavāya*, Vol. I, No. I, 1976, p. 2.

Rūpaṃ Rūpa-vivarjitasya bhavato dhyānena yatkalpitam
Stutyā nirvacanīyatā'khilaguro dūrikṛtā yanmayā
Vyāpitvañca Nirākṛtaṃ Bhagavato yattīrthayātrādinā
Kṣantavyaṃ jagadīśa tadvikalatā doṣatrayam satkṛtam.

CHAPTER V

CONCLUSION

1. *SOME RECENT VIEWS*

(*A*) *The two Brahmans*

In the *Prasthānatraya* as well as in Śaṅkara's commentary, sharp distinction has not been made between the two Brahmans. I have taken the *saguṇa* Brahman to be the *Puruṣottama* or *Vāsudeva* of the *Gītā*, *Īśvara* of the *Brahma-Sūtra* and *Tajjalān* (*Maheśvara*) of the *Upaniṣads*. He is the Supreme Reality who creates this world, sustains it and ultimately destroys it to create it again. He is 'the Goal, the Sustainer, the Lord, the Witness, the Abode, the Shelter and the Friend, the Origin, Dissolution and Stay, the Treasure-house, the Seed imperishable."[1]

He should not be confused with the *nirguṇa* Brahman who is the substratum in which the whole illusory process of *Īśvara* and His creation is superimposed. *Īśvara* is the First Cause whereas Brahman is indescribable...can't be said to be cause or effect of anything.

Failing to understand the significance of the two Brahmans some Western and Indian commentators have mistakenly taken these two Brahmans to be hierarchically arranged...*nirguṇa* Brahman as the higher, *saguṇa* Brahman as the lower. Ninnian Smart has taken the *nirguṇa* Brahman to be the upper deck and

1 A. Mahadeva Sastri, *The BGB*, V. Ramaswamy Sastrulu & Sons, Madras, 1947, p. 249.

Iśvara to be the lower deck.[2] His theory is now-a-days famous as double-decker theory of the Advaita Vedānta. Prof. Mudgal in his book has taken the two Brahmans to be arranged in two tiers.[3]

> The "Two Tier" Philosophy will give a graphic idea of the complete system of Śaṅkara. The upper tier of 'Non-dual' attributeless Brahman, the lower tier of the *Iśvara* and the upper tier of knowledge and freedom, the lower tier of ignorance and bondage, the upper tier of Ens and the lower tier of non-Ens, are clearly implied by the expression "Two Tier" Philosophy. The upper tier is non-empirical, unknowable as an object and yet knowledge itself, transcendental, non-relational, unspeakable, indescribable, inconceivable, beyond thought, beyound words, the realm of Silence, the eternal grand negation, a splendid isolation, a vacuum with no content, without language, and yet is the only light that shines by itself.
>
> The lower tier with a presiding deity, has a warmth of its own. It is an empirical, relational world of knowledge and its objects, spoken, thought about, conceived, described, an affirmation, a multiplicity, a world of hopes and aspirations, of happiness and frustration, subject and object, cause and effect, birth and death, struggle and achievement. Yet, the upper tier is Real and the lower tier is Unreal. The two are unrelated. The lower is nominal, not merely illusory but an illusion. Between these two tiers knowledge serves as an escalator. When knowledge escalates one to the upper tier the lower tier dissolves for that person and the upper tier expands to consume the seeker, who vanishes within it.[4]

However, Mudgal's for that matter, Smart's interpretation of the Advaita Philosophy is clearly wrong. These attempts though neat and clean are not faithful to the *Prasthānatraya* or to Śaṅkara's commentary. Both the phrases, 'two tier' and

2 S. G. Mudgal, *Advaita af Śaṅkara—A Reappraisal*, Motilal Banarsidass, 1975. p. 1.

3 *Ibid.*, p. 2.

4 *Ibid.*, p. 2.

'double-decker' suggest that the two Brahmans belong to the same category of Reality and that is why they can be connected and arranged in a particular way. If one continues one's journey on the ladder then one would reach the lower deck first and then the upper deck or the second tier. But this is not the view which *Prasthānatraya* would support. This view speaks of a Brahman dualism which Śaṅkara's commentary on *Prasthānatraya* would reject at once. In the *Prasthānatraya*, the *nirguṇa* Brahman and *saguṇa* Brahman have been dealt with together, sometimes even in the same *śloka*. The *ślokas* of the *Prāsthānatraya* indicate that they are really two perceptions of the same reality.[5]

The Brahman may be contemplated from two distinct points of view, *svarūpa-lakṣaṇa* and the *taṭastha-lakṣaṇa*. In commenting on I.i.II of the *BSB* Śaṅkara writes that the Brahman is apprehended under two forms—firstly, as qualified by limiting conditions, secondly, as free from all limiting conditions whatsoever. The qualified Brahman is the same as the higher Brahman...*tadeva*. It is qualified by certain names and forms for facilitation of contemplation.[6]

The dualism does not exist at the level of Reality. Only the Brahman is real, everything else is false. But there are two kinds of perceptions...there are two modes of approach to the Reality. The *Prasthānatraya* talks of perception-dualism, not Brahman-dualism. Due to the *saṁskāras*, some people are bestowed with *Yoganiṣṭhā* and they should worship the *saguṇa* Brahman whereas others who possess *Jñānaniṣṭhā* would be able to meditate on the *nirguṇa* Brahman.

(B) Nature of Causality

I have pointed out how *kṣara* is taken to be change or *vināśaśīla* in my thesis. Śaṅkara in his commentary on *Prasthānatraya* has tried to account for the change and to trace out its cause. In Indian Philosophy, ontological, epistemological, logical or ethical issues are not kept separate. One has to find

5 A.G.K. Warrier, *God in Advaita*, Indian Institute of Advanced Study, Simla, 1977, p. 4.

6 *Ibid.*, p. 49.

out the respective implications from the same discussion. I propose to point out the causal implications of Śaṅkara's discussion on *Kṣara*, *Akṣara* and *Puruṣottama*. *Kṣara* suggests *Akṣara*...the cause of *Kṣara*. With Sāṅkhya, Śaṅkara is a *satkāryavādin* for whom the effect pre-exists in the cause. In other words, the *kṣara* pre-existed in *akṣara*. The Manifest was there in subtle form at the unmanifested stage. The difference of Śaṅkara from Sāṅkhya is this, that the Saṅkhya would remain at the stage of *Akṣara* whereas Śaṅkara pushes it back to *Puruṣottama* or *Īśvara*. *Kṣara* and *Akṣara*, both were in *Puruṣottama* and that in the beginning of creation. He creates the Universe out of His *Prakṛti*.[7] Thus, for Śaṅkara, *Puruṣottama* is the First Cause, in the whole cause-effect series of the Universe...the *Aśvattha* tree.

Concepts of the triple *Puruṣas* and the Brahman are landmarks in the search for the ultimate cause by the Vedāntins. In this search, one comes across two theories of causality, the *satkāryavāda* and the *vivartavāda* in the Advaita literature. Many writers have tried to explain this by writing that *satkāryavāda* has two variants...*Pariṇāmavāda* and *Vivartavāda*.[8] Śaṅkara advocated the latter type of *satkāryavāda* whereas, Sāṅkhya and Śrī Rāmānuja adhered to the former type. This sort of solution to the problem has failed to grasp the essential difference between *satkāryavāda* and *vivartavāda*.

Satkāryavāda and *Asatkāryavāda* can be taken to be two views of causality and it is true that Vedānta Subscribed to the *Satkāryavāda*. For the *Satkāryavāda*, the effect pre-exists in the cause. For the *Asatkāryavāda*,the effect exists independent of the cause. Many think that *Pariṇāmevāda* or which says that the effect is actual transformation is a kind of *Satkāryavāda* is opposed to the view of *vivartavāda* which says that effect is a mere appearance.

7 S. Radhakrishnan, *The Principal Upaniṣads*, George Allen and Unwin Ltd, London, 1953, p. 449.

8 M. C. Bhartiya, *Causation in Indian Philosophy*, Vimal Prakshan, Ramnagar, Ghaziabad, U.P., 1973, p 9.

But *Vivartavāda* is not a theory of causality but a cancellation of it.[9] It has been formulated to point out the relationship of Brahman with the triple *puruṣas*. It can't be said to be the cause of *Īśvara*, *Akṣara* and *Kṣara* as Brahman is indescribable. In the causal sequence, *Īśvara* is taken to be the First Cause. There can't be a cause of the First Cause. Brahman is the *adhiṣṭhāna* because of which the illusion of the triple *puruṣas* arose. But *adhiṣṭhāna* is not a cause. The superimposition or *adhyāsa* needs a basis...the basis here is the Brahman.

Thus, Vedānta's teaching on causality is very modern. Causality can be taken to be a principle which is being applied in the knowledge-game because it pays or works in the *vyavahārika-sattā*. This *vyavahārika-sattā* leads us to *Īśvara* whom one should worship, seek His help. He has transformed himself and become in part the whole Universe.

> The *BS* '*ātmakṛteḥ pariṇāmāt*' suggests an actual transformation of God into the world, extended in space and time. Śaṅkara admits that a preliminary formulation of causality in Advaita makes use of the idea of an actual transformation of cause into effect, of God into the world.[10]

So it is *Satkāryavāda* and *Pariṇāmavāda*. Some people may by temperament be fit to go so far and view causality in this way. But that causality belongs to reality is not a fact.

9 S.R. Bhatta, *Studies in Rāmānuja Vedānta*, Heritage Publishers, New Delhi, 1975, p. 92.

"Transcendentally speaking, causation has no value in Śaṅkara's Philosophy, because for him identity is the only truth. Yet for phenomenal purposes he accepts its value and makes a synthesis of causation with identity, the result of which is the doctrine of *Vivartavāda*, which simultaeously accepts and denies causation. In fact, it is a denial rather than acceptance of causation. Brahman does not stand in a causal relation with anyone, because it is the only Reality, causation is the necessity of thought but identity transcends thought."

A.G.R. Warrier almost agrees with this view in his book *God in Advaita* (p. 105). However these thinkers fail to notice that in giving these views on causation Śaṅkara is anticidating the modern view that causality does not belong to reality but it is merely a leading principle.

10 A.G.K. Warrier, *God in Advaita*, Indian Institute of Advanced Study, Simla, 1977, p. 106.

Therefore, in sober truth, that concept is irrational, points out Śaṅkara—*paramārthatastu na kasyacid kenacidapi prakāreṇa kāryakāraṇabhāva upapadyate.* The Advaitic truth is that for the sage there is neither *māyā* nor causality.[11]

In modern terminology, causality or the causal principle is "neither true nor false, for it is not a statement (proposition) about the world at all. Rather, it exprrsses a resolve, 'Let us find uniformities in the world.' It is sometimes called a *leading principle* because it leads or guides us in our empirical investigations."[12]

All this Śaṅkara has suggested in his commentaries on the *Prasthānatraya.*

(C) Dahara-ākāśa

In many *Upaniṣads*, the *Brahma-Sūtra* and the *Gītā* mention of *Dahara-ākāśa* has been made which has led to many mystic explanations. Furthermore, the question regarding the nature of *Dahara Puruṣa* has been debated upon by philosophers. I have taken *Dahara Puruṣa* to be *Īśvara* or *saguṇa* Brahman in my thesis. It is because the *Dahara Puruṣa* in these *ślokas* has been taken to be the sustainer of this universe *i.e.*, He is connected with the Universe, which logically makes him the *saguṇa* Brahman. Thus *Dahara Puruṣa* is *Puruṣottama* for me. The *Upaniṣads* ask everybody to seek after this *Dahara-Puruṣa* and to understand Him. It is the solemn duty and destiny of man. The *BU* asserts, "*ātmā vā are draṣṭavyaḥ...nididhyāsitavyaḥ*".[13] Śaṅkara's discussion regarding the nature of Brahman as the meaning of *Dahara Puruṣa* is ambiguous. He writes... "the *Yogins* perceive that Brahman, pure, appearing like the light of consciousness...*vijñānajyotiḥ svarūpāvabhāsaṁ tāvanmātraṁ brahmopalabhyata.*"[14] This indicates the *nirguṇa* Brah-

11 S.R. Bhatta, *Studies in* Rāmānuja Vedānta, p. 108.

12 John Hospers, *An Introduction to Philosophical Analysis*, Prentice-Hall, Inc., Englewond Cliffa, N.J., 1964, p. 261.

13 S. Radhakrishnan, *The Principal Upaniṣads*, George Allen and Unwin Ltd., London, 1953, p. 197.

14 *Śaṅkarabhāṣya*, Gītā Press, Gorakhpur, p. 809.

man. But he also writes that all His desires are infallible. His volitions arising out of those desires are also true. In the case of God both desires and volitions are due to the limitations of pure *sattva*...*"saṅkalpāḥ kāmāśca śuddhasattvopādhinimitta īśvarasya."*[15] Thus, Śaṅkara's discussions mention of both these Brahmans because one can meditate on any of these Brahmans according to one's taste and *niṣṭhā*. However, when one relates the Brahman to the body...the world, where there is talk of any limitations, then one is logically bound to point out to the *saguṇa* Brahman.

A literal interpretation of the city of Brahman, '*Brahma-pura*'...white lotus in the heart (*hṛdaya-puṇḍarīka*) and the *Dahara-ākāśa* would lead to absurdity. However, people have accepted it in this literal way and mystics and the *Yogins* have been practising meditation in this way. But Śaṅkara takes all these attempts to understand the passage to be attempts of feeble-minded persons. The *Upaniṣad* has given it in this way for the benefit of the duller-persons only...*"mandabuddhīnāṁ... tadadhigamāya hṛdaya-puṇḍarīkadeśa upadeṣṭavyāḥ."*[16] He gives a reasoned explanation of this passage of the *Chāndogya* and other *Upaniṣads*. For him, the whole discussion is a pointer to the possibilities of realising Brahman by applying one's reason (*hṛdaya*).

The reasoning suggested is definitely to analyse the change or *kṣara*, to pass on from *kṣara* to *akṣara* and from *akṣara* to *Puruṣottama*. But whether independent reasoning would lead one to *Puruṣottama* or not is an open question. According to Śaṅkara, *hṛdaya* or 'reasoning' should be exercised with the help of the teacher or hearing of the scriptures...*"gurvāśraya-śravaṇādyupāyairanviṣya ca sākṣātkaraṇīyanityārthaḥ."*[17]

The most important philosophical point suggested by Śaṅkara is the categorical difference between the object of philosophical enquiry...the Brahman, and the body or the physical heart. *"...badarmātraṁ kimapi vidyate kiṁ tasyānve-*

15 *Śaṅkarabhāṣya*, Gītā Press, Gorakhpur, p. 817.

16 *Ibid.*, p. 803.

17 *Ibid.*, p. 807.

ṣaṇena vijihāsituḥ syāt"[18]—what results the seekers should get even if they find some objects inside the heart. In other words, if the Brahman would be a mere object like other objects, then how does it solve our philosophical problems ?

In his commentary on the Gītā Śaṅkara takes this sort of knowledge to be *Tāmasic.* Only beings who do not possess faculty of discrimination take *Īśvara* to be an object, the mere stone or piece of wood, the material of which the image is made. The fallacy here consists of "clinging to one single effect as if it were all" (*BGB* 18.22).

(D) *The Highest Ethical Person*

Dr. Ganeswar Misra has taken *Puruṣottama* to be the highest ethical person in his book '*The Advaita Conception of Philosophy : Its Method, Scope and Limits.*'

> The highest ethical person *Puruṣottama* who has completely overcome his passions, who is not actuated by any motive of personal loss and gain, in otherwords who is an *Āptakāma* like Lord *Vāsudeva*, will perform his duty out of pure regard for moral law. A *Kṣatriya* who performs the duties of a *Kṣatriya* is still a regional man having an ego-sense of belonging to a particular region. Here he is still under the spell of an ego-sense, considering himself as he does as a *Brahmin* or a *Kṣatriya* or a *Śūdra* or a father or a husband, etc. But a *Puruṣottama* or a purely ethical person is one who has overcome his limited ego-sense does not identify himself as of this or that class or of this or that kin or of any class or kind whatsoever. One, who no longer classifies himself as belonging to this or that class has completely merged himself and lost his identity in the Universal life. Being above the duties attaching to particular station which generates and strengthens the ego-sense one becomes completely free as a moral agent. At that time he is completely free from passion, interest and desires and works for the general good. When one is working for the general good and not for the

18 *Śaṅkarabhāṣya* Gītā Press Gorakhpu p. 801.

good of this or that class he has no passions. He does not come into conflict with any body, does not encouter any opposition and has no occasion to feel himself as distinct from others.[19]

Similar views have been expressed by others also.

But the whole view stands on a misconception of the term *Puruṣottama*. *Puruṣottama* does not mean the person who is superior to others because of his ethical qualities. It means the *Puruṣa* who controls the other two *puruṣas*, who has originated these two and who sustains them and would destroy them at the end of the *kalpa* to create them anew. The comparision is not between human beings but between the types of realities. Popularly speaking, *Puruṣottama* has the sense in which Dr. G. Misra has taken like the *Marjyādā Puruṣottama*. But in the philosophical treatise it is being used in a different sense as I have pointend out before.

The *Puruṣottama* is linked with the society as He incarnates himself when the *dharma* degenerates. Śaṅkara writes in his Introduction to the *Bhagāvadgītā* :

> When, owing to the ascendancy of lust in its votaries, religion was overpowered by irreligion caused by the vanishing faculty of discrimination, and irreligion was advancing, it was then that the original Creator *(Adi-katṛ)*, *Viṣṇu*, known as *Nārāyaṇa*, wishing to maintain order in the Universe, incarnated Himself as *Kṛṣṇa*, begotten in *Devakī* by *Vāsudeva*, for the preservation of the 'earthly Brahman' of spiritual life *(Brāhmaṇatva)* on the earth. For it was by the preservation of spiritual life that the *Vedic* Religion could be preserved, since thereon depend all distinctions of caste and religious order. The Lord always possessed as He is of

19 G. Misra, *Advaita Conception of Philosophy: Its Method, Scope and Limits*, Utkal University Campus, Bhubaneswar, 1976, p. 133.

"Logically and psychologically God is man at his best, writ large, the Universalization and maximization of the human spirit." (Quoted from A.G.K. Warrier's book *God in Advaita*, p. 7.)

Such views are attempts to reduce religious language to ethical language. They display a kind of reductionism.

(infinite) knowledge, supremacy, power, strength, might and vigour, controls the *Māyā*—belonging to Him as *Viṣṇu*,—the *Mūla-Prakṛti*, the First Cause, composed of three *Guṇas* or energies, and He appears to the world as though He is born and embodied and helping the world at large; whereas really He is unborn and indestructible, is the Lord of creatures, and is by nature Eternal, Pure, Intelligent and Free.[20]

These comments by Śaṅkara clearly show where Dr. Misra's thesis has gone wrong. He has failed to distinguish a *Sthitaprajña* and the *Puruṣottama*. The *Puruṣottama* is the God Himself whereas an *Avatāra* may posses all the qualities as discussed by Dr. G. Misra. The *Sthitaprajña* is a person who has attained wisdom in steady contemplation (*samādhiprajña*). A description of the characteristics of this Sage has been given from *BGB* II.55 to the end of the Discourse. An *Avatāra* is a divine descent whereas *Sthitaprajña* is an ascent, a realized soul. The *Gītā* stresses the speciality of an *Avatāra* as follows: "Whoso knows thus My divine birth and action in truth is not born again on leaving this body; he comes to me, O Arjuna."[21]

Śaṅkara comments on it that an *Avatāra's* birth is an illusion (*Māyā*). "It is Divine, peculiar to *Īśvara*, not of ordinary nature (*aprākṛta*)."[22] And both should not be confused with *Puruṣottama* who possesses the capacity to create, sustain and destroy the Universe. However, *Sthitaprajña* and the *Avatāra* can be taken to be highest ethical persons, but never the *Puruṣottama*. Ethicality or morality suggests imperfection, struggle, limitation in knowledge, choice whereas these concepts would not be applicable in the case of the lord. This has been forcefully suggested in the 22nd *śloka* of 3rd *adhyāya* of the *Gītā*:

> I have nothing whatsoever to achieve in the three worlds, O son of *Pṛthā*, nor is there anything unattained that should be attained, yet I engage in action.[23]

20 A. Mahadeva Sastri, *The BGB*, V. Ramaswamy Sastrulu & Sons, Madras, 1947, p. 2-3.

21 *Ibid.*, p. 122.

22 *Ibid.*, p. 122.

23 *Ibid.*, p. 106.

2. CHARACTERISTICS OF THE PURUṢOTTAMA

Now I wish to gather togerther and develop some hints that have been dropped in previous pages about the *Puruṣottama*. As I have pointed out before, *Puruṣottama* is compared with the other two *Puruṣas*, i.e., *Kṣara* and *Akṣara*. In relation to them it is *Uttama*. I pointed out how a misunderstanding of this term *uttama* led a scholar like G. Misra in the wrong track.

The adjective *uttama* is not used with reference to any single charateristic or property. Perhaps this adjectival term qualifying the *Puruṣa* stands for a variety of properties and characteristics, all related to one another in different ways. I shall suggest some of these properties...shall trace out some of the "family resemblances" among these in regard to the *Puruṣa*. In doing this, I shall mainly depend on Śaṅkara's commentary on the *Gītā* though these have their corresponding points in his commentary on the *Upaniṣads* and the *Brahma-Sūtra*.

Uttama is that which is absolutely real (*vastu sat*). *Kṣara* is unreal as it is an effect and every effect is unreal and so also is *akṣara*.

> Thus, every effect is unreal, because it is not perceived as distinct from its cause. Every effect, such as pot, is unreal, also because it is not perceived before its production and after its destruction.[24]

Uttama can be understood in the sence of possessing *śakti* or control. *Māyā* is the power of the Lord (*Parameśa-śakti*). It is to be noted that this concept of power distinguishes the Vedāntic conception of *Māyā* from the Sāṅkhya view of *Prakṛti*. *Puruṣottama* controls the other two *Puruṣas*. It is said, "*Kṣaraḥ sarvāṇi bhūtāni*" and then has been said... "*Bhrāmayan sarvabhūtāni yantrārūḍhāni māyayā.*" The Lord causes all beings to revolve as if...mounted on machine.[25] God is the First Cause. He is *Puruṣottama* in this sense. He causes the other two *Puruṣas* to came into existence. They are created, maintained and destroyed by His will.

24 A. Mahadeva Sastri, *The BGB*, V. Ramaswamy Sastralu & Sons, Madras, 1947, p. 34.

25 *Ibid.*, p. 497.

All beings, O son of Kuntī, go into My *Prakṛti* at the end of a *kalpa*. I send them forth again at the beginning of (the next) *kalpa*.[26]

I am the father of this world, the mother, the dispensor, the grandsire; I am the knowable, the Purifier, the syllable '*Om*', and also the *Ṛk*, the *Sāman*, and the *Yajus* also.[27]

Śaṅkara usually takes causes to be superior to the effects. In that sense he, in *VC*, takes *Māyā* to be superior to the effects.[28]

Uttama can be understood in the sense of Lordship. And a lord is one "in whom the six attributtes of unimpeded dominion etc., ever abide collectively and in perfection and who possesses a complete knowledge of the Origin of the Universe etc., says the *VP*.

'*Bhaga*' means the six attributes—perfect dominion, might, glory, splendour, dispassion and salvation. (vi 5-75)

He is called the Lord (*Bhagavat*) who knows the origin and the end, the coming and going of beings, what is wisdom and what is ignorance.[29] (vi 5-78)

Puruṣottama is identical with the Brahman. Śaṅkara has addressed Him in that way in many of his *ślokas* : "I bow to *Govinda* whose nature is Bliss Supreme, who is the *Sadguru*, who can be known only from the import of all Vedānta and who is beyond the reach of speech and mind."[30] Denotationally they point out the same thing. Śaṅkara writes that "Brahman exists as *Īśvara* or the Lord of the Universe."[31] "Thou art the Imperishable, the Supreme Being worthy to be known."[32] But

26 A Mahadeva Sastri, *The BGB*, V. Ramaswamy Sastrulu & Sons, Madras, 1947, p. 243.

27 *Ibid.*, p. 249.

28 *Vivekacūḍāmaṇi of Śrī Śaṅkarācārya*, Advaita Ashrama, Calcutta, 1974, p, 39.

29 A. Mahadeva Sastri, *The BGB*, V. Ramaswamy Sastrulu & Sons, Madras, p. 114.

30 Swami Madhavananda, *Vivakachudamani*, p. 30.

31 A. Mahadeva Sastri, *The BGB*. p. 348.

32 *Ibid.*, p. 283.

meditation on the Imperishable is difficult as it is devoid of all conditions and beyond all speech and thought.

> Greater is their trouble whose thoughts are set on the Unmanifest; for, the Goal, the Unmanifest, is very hard for the embodied to reach.[33]

Hence, Arjuna is advised to practice *Karma-Yoga*. The Lord dewells in the hearts of all beings and one should take refuse in Him, the *Dahara Puruṣa*.

Puruṣottama appears to be born and embodied through His own *Māyā*, but not in reality, unlike others. The occasion for such embodiment arises whenever there is a decay of *dharma* i.e., decay and corruption in the institution of castes and religious orders which are the means of attaining wordly prosperity and salvation.

> For the protection of the good for the destruction of evil-doers, for the firm establishment of religion, I am born in every age.[34]

Puruṣottama is not the only word used in the *Gītā* to indicate the *Īśvara*. He is also addressed as *Sanātnna Puruṣa*, *Ādya Puruṣa* or *Puruṣa Purāṇa*. But they are philosophically not as important as the term *Puruṣottama*.

33 A Mahadeva Sastri, *The BGB*, V. Ramaswamy Systrulu & Sons, Madras, p. 345.

34 *Ibid.*, p. 122.

BIBLIOGRAPHY

(A) *PRIMARY SOURCES*:

1. Gambhirananda, Swami. *Eight Upaniṣads*, 2v., Advaita Ashrama, Calcutta, 1972.
2. ———— *Brahma-Sūtra-Bhāṣya of Śrī Śaṅkarācārya*, Advaita Ashrama, Calcutta, 1972.
3. Śaṅkarabhāṣya. *Vedānta Darśana*, Gītā Press, Gorakhpur, Saṃvat 2012.
4. ———— *Śrīmad Bhagavad-Gītā*, Gītā Press, Gorakhpur, Saṃvat 2024.
5. ———— *Śvetāśvatara and other Upaniṣads*, Gītā Press, Gorakhpur, Saṃvat 2016.
6. ———— *Chāndogya Upaniṣad*, Gītā Press, Gorakhpur, Samvat 2019.
7. Sastri, A. Mahadeva., *The Bhagavad-Gītā with the commentary of Śrī Śaṅkarācārya*, V. Ramaswamy Sastrulu & Sons, Madras, 1947.

(B) *SECONDARY SOURCES*:

1. Aurobindo, Sri. *Essays on the Gītā*, New York, 1950.
2. Belvalkar, S.K. & Ranade, R. D. *History of Indian Philosophy, The Creative Period*, Orient Book Reprint Corporation, New Delhi, 1955.
3. Beidler, William. *The Vision of Self in Early Vedānta*, Motilal Banarsidass, Delhi, 1975.
4. Bhatt, S.R. *Studies in Rāmānuja Vedānta*, Heritage Publishers, New Delhi, 1975.
5. Bhattacharyya, K. C. *Studies in Vedāntism*, University of Calcutta, Calcutta, 1909.
6. Bhartiya, M. C. *Causation in Indian Philosophy*, Vimal Prakashan, Ramanagar, Ghaziabad, U.P., 1973.
7. Chatterjee, S.C. *The Wisdom of the Vedas*, Vikas Publishing House Pvt. Ltd., New Delhi, 1975.

8. Chatterjee, S. C. *Classical Indian Philosophies : Their Synthesis in the Philosophy of Sri Ramakrishna*, University of Calcutta, Calcutta, 1963.
9. Das, Nilakantha: *Śrīmad Bhagavad Gītā*, New Students Store, Cuttack, 1968.
10. Deutsch, Eliot. *Advaita Vedānta : A Philosophical Recontruction*, East-West Centre Press, Honolulu, 1969.
11. Deussen, Paul. *The System of the Vedānta*, Leipzig, 1883.
12. ———— *The Philosophy of the Upaniṣads*, Edinburgh, 1906.
13. Dutta, D.M. *Six Ways of Knowing*, University of Calcutta, Calcutta, 1960.
14. Hiriyana, M. *Outlines of Indian Philosophy*, George Allen & Unwin, London, 1973.
15. ———— *Essentials of Indian Philosophy*, George Allen & Unwin, London, 1959.
16. Hill, W.D.P. *The Bhagavad-Gītā*, Oxford, 1847.
17. Hospers, John. *An Introduction to Philosophical Analysis*, Prentice Hall, Inc., Englewood Cliffs, N. J., 1964.
18. Hume, R. E. *Thirteen Principal Upaniṣads*, Oxford University, 1949.
19. Iyer, M. K. Venkataraman. *Advaita Vedānta*, Asia Publishing House, New York, 1964.
20. Jagadananda, Swami. *Upadeśasāhaśrī of Śrī Śaṅkarācārya*, Sri Ramakrishna Math, Madras, 1961.
21. Jha, G. *Śaṅkara Vedānta*, Mahārājādhirāja Śrī Rameshwara Singh Bahadur of Durbhanga Lecture Series, Vol.I., 1939.
22. Johnston, E. H. *Early Sāṅkhya*, Royal Asiatic Society, London, 1937.
23. Joshi, N.V. *The Three Fountainheads of Indian Philosophy*, Somaiya Publications, Pvt. Ltd. Bombay, 1972.
24. Keith, A. B. *The Philosophy and Religion of the Veda and the Upanishads*, Harvard University Press, Cambridge, Massachussetts, 1925 (Harvard Oriental Series, Vol. XXXII)
25. Madhavananda, Swami. *Minor Upaniṣads*, Advaita Ashrama, Calcutta, 1968.

26. ———— *Vivekacūḍāmaṇi of Śrī Śaṅkarācārya*, Advaita Ashrama, Calcutta, 1974.
27. Mahadevan, T.M.P. *The Philosophy of Advaita*, Luzac and Co., London 1938.
28. Maitra, S. K. *The Main Problems of Philosophy* (Part II), Progressive Publishers, Calcutta, 1962.
29. Max Muller, F. *The Six Systems of Indian Philosophy*, Associated Publishing House, New Delhi, 1973.
30. Mehta, P. D. *Early Indian Religious Thought*, Luzac and Company Ltd., London, 1956.
31. Misra, G. *The Advaita Conception of Philosophy : Its Method, Scope and Limits*, Utkal University Campus, Bhubaneswar, 1976.
32. Modi, P. M. *Akṣara—A Forgotten Chapter in the History of Indian Philosophy*, Baroda State Press, Baroda, 1932.
33. Monier-Williams, M. *Indian Wisdom (The Chawkhamba Sanskrit Studies, Vol. XXXVI)*, Chowkhamba Sanskrit Series Office, Varanasi 1963.
34. Mudgal, S. G. *Advaita of Saṅkara—A Reappraisal*, Moti Lal Banarsidass, Delhi, 1975.
35. Murty, K. S. *Revelation and Reason in Advaita Vedānta*, Columbia University Press, New York, 1961.
36. Murty, T. R. V. *The Central Philosophy of Buddhism*, George Allen & Unwin, London, 1955.
37. Nikhilananda, Swami. *The Upaniṣads*, Phoenix House Ltd., London, W. C. 2, 1957.
38. Ninnian Smart. *Doctrine and Argument in Indian Philosophy*, George Allen & Unwin, London, 1964.
39. Potter, Karl. *Presuppositions of India's philosophies*, Prentice-Hall, Inc. Englewood Cliffs, New Jersey, 1963.
40. Prithipal, D. *Advaita Vedanta*, Bharatiya Vidya Prakashan, Varanasi, 1969.
41. Radhakrishnan, S. *Indian Philosophy*, Vol. I, George Allen and Unwin, 1948.
42. ———— *Indian Philosophy*. Vol. II, George Allen and Unwin, 1958.
43. ———— *The Bhagavad-Gītā*, George Allen & Unwin, London, 1948.

44. ——— *The Principal Upaniṣads*, George Allen & Unwin Ltd., New York, 1953.
45. ——— *The Brahma-Sūtras*, George Allen & Unwin Ltd., London, 1960.
46. Ranade, R.D. *A Constructive Survey of Indian Philosophy*, Oriental Book Agency, Poona, 1926.
47. Reyna, Ruth. *Introduction to Indian Philosophy*, Tata Mac Graw-Hill Publishing Co. Ltd., New Delhi, 1971.
48. ——— *The Concept of Māyā from the Vedas to the 20th Century*, Asia Publishing House, New Delhi, 1962.
49. Roy, D. P. *The Bhagavad Gītā—a revelation*, Indian Book Company, New Delhi, 1974.
50. Saksena, S.K. *Nature of Consciousness in Hindu Philosophy* Motilal Banarsidass, Delhi, 1971.
51. Sampatkumar, M. R. *Gītābhāṣya of Rāmānuja*, Vidya Press, Madras, 1st Edition, 1969.
52. Sengupta, Anima. *A Critical Study of the Philosophy of Rāmānuja*, The Chowkhamba Sanskrit Series, Varanasi, 1967.
53. Sharma, B. R. *The Concept of Ātman in lhe Principal Upaniṣads*, Dinesh Publications, New Delhi, 1972.
54. Sharma, C. D. *A Critical Survey of Indian Philosophy*, Motilal Banarsidass, 1964.
55. Singh, Balbir. *The Conceptual Framework of Indian Philosophy*, The Macmillan Company of India Ltd., Delhi, 1976.
56. Sircar, M. N. *Hindu Mysticism*, Bharatiya Mahavidyalaya, Calcutta, 1943.
57. Swahananda, Swami. *The Chāndogya Upaniṣad*, 1st Edition, Ramakishna Math Publications, Madras, 1956.
58. Tilak, B. G. *Śrīmad Bhagavad Gītā Rahaṣya*, Lokamanya Tilak Mandir, Poona, 1903.
59. Upadhyaya, K. N. *Early Buddhism and Bhagavad Gītā* Motilal Banarsidass, Delhi, 1971.
60. Warrier, A. G. K. *God in Advaita*, Indian Institute of Advanced Study, Simla, 1977.

INDEX